Ian Venables

ELEGY

for violoncello and piano

NOVELLO

Programme note:

The Elegy for 'Cello and Piano Op. 2 was the first piece written by the composer for solo instrument and piano. Written in 1980 for the 'cellist Anthony Gammage, it is as an elegy for an unreturned love, and has all the melodic and harmonic fingerprints of Venables's mature style: combining tender lyricism with passionate intensity. Strong uncompromising chords open the work, above which an angular melody is intoned, presaging the work's main thematic material. The 'cello's plangent outpouring, accompanied by sorrow-laden chords, leads to a central chorale – described by one reviewer as "...a passage of overwhelming beauty." After a restatement of the earlier section, a short cadenza for the 'cello ushers in the work's main climax, where both instruments present the earlier piano introduction, before plummeting towards its final chord: the prevailing b minor tonality assailed by the 'cello's A-sharp as it acts out an aural metaphor on the pain of unrequited love.

Duration: 7 minutes

for
Anthony Gammage

Elegy

Ian Venables Op. 2

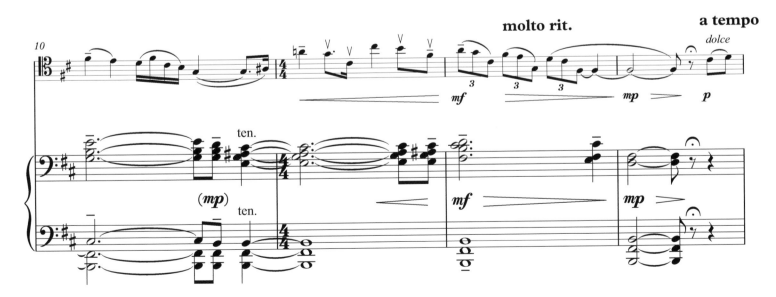

Ian Venables

ELEGY

for violoncello and piano

NOVELLO

Elegy

Ian Venables Op. 2

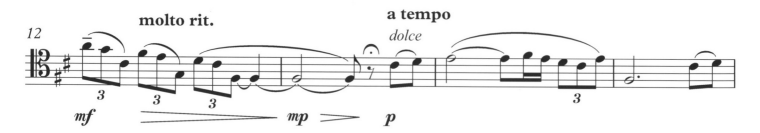

molto rit.

20

_f_   **mf** _sub._

a tempo ma semplice

23   _lunga_

mp   (**mp**)

allarg.   **a tempo**

26

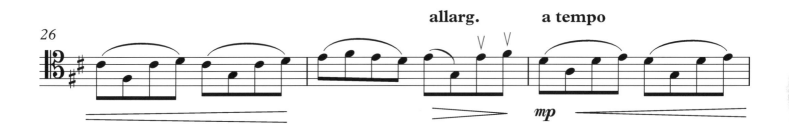

mp

poco rall.   **a tempo**

29

_f_   **mp** _dolce_

31

34   _dolcissimo_   Sul D   _poco_
ten.

pp _sub._   **mp**

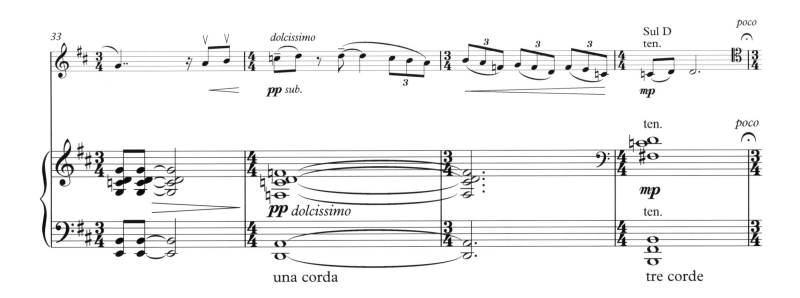

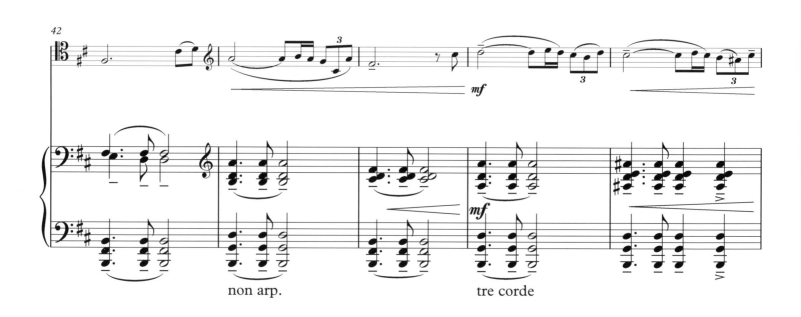

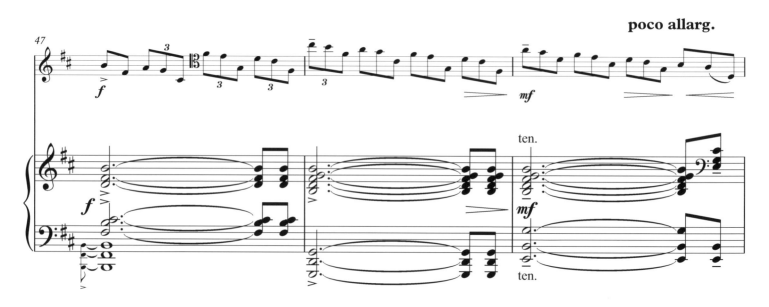

Published by
Novello Publishing Limited
14-15 Berners Street,
London W1T 3LJ, UK.

Exclusive Distributors:
Music Sales Limited
Distribution Centre, Newmarket Road,
Bury St Edmunds, Suffolk IP33 3YB, UK.

Order No. NOV164219
ISBN 978-1-78305-608-8

Cover illustration by Anthony Gill.

Printed in the EU.

www.musicsalesclassical.com

Discover th

NORTH
YORK MOORS

Photograph and artwork acknowledgements

David Daly (bird artworks): pages 12, 22, 24, 28, 34, 36, 48, 54, 60

Mike Kipling: Contents page, pages 7, 10, 24, 25, 27, 45, 62, 63

Chris Ceaser: Contents page, pages 20, 22, 25, 45, 47, 53

John Knight: Contents page, pages 14, 59

Roger Dalladay: pages 29, 52, 61

Mark Denton: Front Cover, Title page, Contents page, pages 15, 29, 30, 33, 44,

Tony Bartholomew: Contents page, pages 25, 26, 33, 37, 43, 46, 48, 49, 52, 55, 58, 59

Tony Bartholomew's photographs of artefacts from

Whitby Museum on the following pages, are by kind permission of Whitby Museum: pages 16, 23, 26, 34, 35, 39, 43, 57

Robin Lidster: page 36

Blaise Vyner: page 36

Brian Nellist: page 14

John Burden: page 60

Pannett Park Art Gallery, Whitby: page 33

National Archives: page 39

The Hayes Collection, Ryedale Folk Museum: page 46

Gillies Jones Glass: page 47

Forestry Commission: page 48

All other photographs are from the collection of the North York Moors National Park Authority.

First published by North York Moors National Park Authority, 2007. Revised 2012

Copyright © Roger Osborne 2007

Roger Osborne has asserted his right under the Copyright, Designs and Patents Act, 1988 to be identified as the author of this work

North York Moors National Park Authority
The Old Vicarage
Bondgate
Helmsley
York YO62 5BP
Tel 01439 772700

A CIP catalogue record for this book is available from the British Library

ISBN 978-1-904622-13-0

Designed by Alan Marshall

MIX
Paper from
responsible sources
FSC® C004309
www.fsc.org

WORLD
LAND
TRUST™
www.carbonbalancedpaper.com
CBP0001013200812083

Discover the
NORTH YORK MOORS

ROGER OSBORNE

THE OFFICIAL GUIDE TO THE
NORTH YORK MOORS NATIONAL PARK

CONTENTS

The
NORTH YORK MOORS

Welcome to the North York Moors National Park, one of Britain's most beautiful landscapes. This guide will show you many of the delights that this extraordinary place has to offer, and should encourage you to get out and experience it for yourself. The North York Moors is an area of great natural beauty, but is also a living landscape, marked by thousands of years of human history and still full of change and activity.

The central feature of the National Park is the unbroken area of heather moorland, stretching for 50 kilometres from Osmotherley to the North Sea coast. Cut into the high central moorland is a series of dales, and the contrast between the open moorland and the sweeping green pastures of the dales is one of the most captivating sights the English countryside has to offer.

The central uplands are flanked on all sides by spectacular landforms. To the south lie the Tabular Hills with forests and wooded dales; to the west, a steep escarpment; to the north, the majestic sweep of the Cleveland Hills; and to the east there are the magnificent cliffs, bays and beaches of the Yorkshire coast.

The moorland, woods, rivers and coast provide habitats for a wide range of mammals, birds, reptiles, insects, trees, fungi, and flowers and, while many of these are given special protection, there are plenty of opportunities to see and enjoy the extraordinary wildlife.

The North York Moors is special for another reason. Humans first came to live in this area around 8 to 9,000 years ago. Early inhabitants cleared forests and left barrows and cairns across the moors, while later Iron Age people created hill forts and systems of boundary dykes. For the Romans this was a dangerous frontier, requiring forts and signal stations.

ABOVE: *Young Ralph cross stands on Blakey Ridge near the centre of the moors, and is the emblem of the North York Moors National Park.*
OPPOSITE: *The heather moorland and sweeping dales provide a vivid contrast.*

Centuries later, monks came to build great abbeys, putting up crosses and laying trackways across the moorland. From the 17th to 19th centuries iron, jet and alum mining transformed the landscape, leaving a host of industrial relics.

A unique attraction of the North York Moors is that, because urban sprawl and mechanised farming has left the moors largely unaffected, the whole of this history is plainly visible. As well as a beautiful landscape, the moors offer a wonderful lesson in human history. Recent history is here too, as local customs, building styles, folk-tales and dialect flourish. Many artists find inspiration in the landscape and its people.

The North York Moors National Park was created to conserve this unique environment. But time does not stand still; the National Park Authority is continually finding ways to improve the relation between landscape and people through education, sustainable tourism, environmental research, better access, public transport and sensitive planning. As we rediscover the importance of the natural world then, far from being a window on the past, the North York Moors is a model for the future.

This short guide gives you a flavour of this beautiful place. The moors are for everyone to enjoy, and the book provides lots of ideas for walking, riding and cycling, as well as routes for wheelchair users. The National Park is crossed by two of the most scenic railway lines in Britain. For more information on public transport, access and a host of other topics, including leaflets on walks mentioned in the book, see the section at the end of this book, or visit the website at www.northyorkmoors.org.uk. And, most important of all, take the opportunity to get out and enjoy this remarkable place.

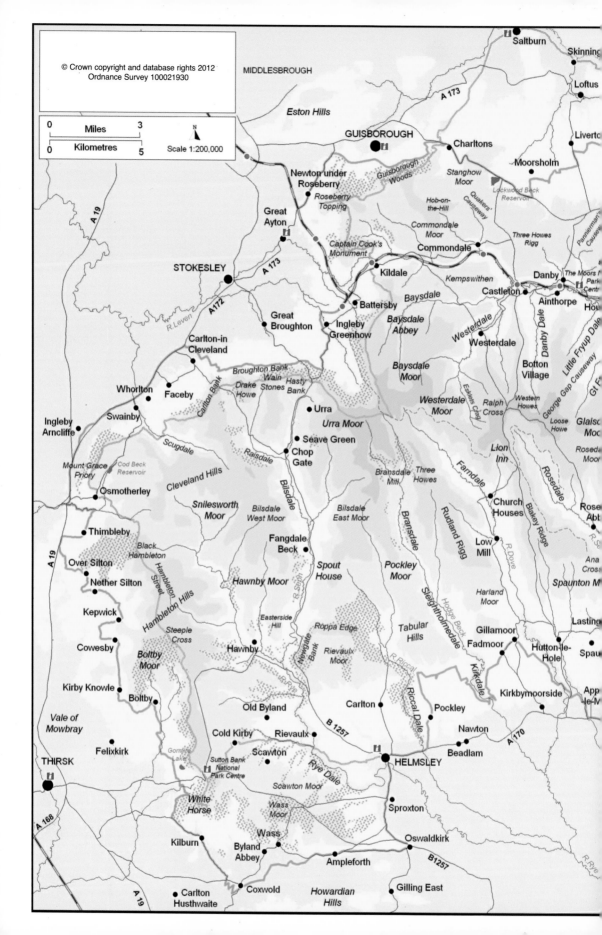

MIDDLESBROUGH

Miles 0 — 3
Kilometres 0 — 5
Scale 1:200,000
N

A 19

A 173

Eston Hills

GUISBOROUGH

Charltons

Guisborough Woods

Stanghow Moor

Moorsholm

Saltburn

Skinning

Loftus

Liverto

Liverton

Newton under Roseberry

Roseberry Topping

Hob-on-the-Hill

Lockwood Beck Reservoir

Quakers Causeway

Parnerman's Causewa

Great Ayton

Captain Cook's Monument

Commondale Moor

Three Howes Rigg

Kildale

Commondale

Danby

The Moors Park Centre

STOKESLEY

A 173

A 172

Battersby

Baysdale

Kempswithen

Castleton

Ainthorpe

Hou

R. Leven

Great Broughton

Ingleby Greenhow

Baysdale Abbey

Westerdale

Westerdale

Danby Dale

Little Fryup Dale

Carlton-in-Cleveland

Broughton Bank
Wain Stones
Hasty Bank

Baysdale Moor

Gt F

George Gap Causeway

Whorlton

Faceby

Carlton Bank

Drake Howe

Urra

Westerdale Moor

Eskers Crag

Ralph Cross

Western Howes

Loose Howe

Glaisc Moc

Swainby

Urra Moor

Seave Green

Lion Inn

Rosede Moor

Ingleby Arncliffe

Scugdale

Raisdale

Chop Gate

Bransdale Mill

Three Howes

Farndale

Mount Grace Priory

Cod Beck Reservoir

Cleveland Hills

Bilsdale

Church Houses

Rosed Abl

Osmotherley

Snilesworth Moor

Bilsdale West Moor

Bilsdale East Moor

Bransdale

Rudland Rigg

R. Dove

Blakey Ridge

Rosedale

Thimbleby

Black Hambleton

Fangdale Beck

Spout House

Pockley Moor

Low Mill

Ana Cross

Spaunton M

Over Silton

Nether Silton

Hambleton Street

Hawnby Moor

R. Seph

Harland Moor

Kepwick

Hambleton Hills

Easterside Hill

Roppa Edge

Tabular Hills

Gillamoor

Lasting

Cowesby

Steeple Cross

Hawnby

Rievaulx Moor

Fadmoor

Hutton-le-Hole

Spau

Kirby Knowle

Boltby Moor

Newgate Bank

R. Rye

R. Riccal

Sleightholmedale

Hodge Beck

Kirkbymoorside

App -le-M

Boltby

Old Byland

Carlton

Pockley

Vale of Mowbray

Cold Kirby

Rievaulx

Riccal Dale

Nawton

A 170

Beadlam

Felixkirk

Gormire Lake

Scawton

B 1257

HELMSLEY

THIRSK

Sutton Bank National Park Centre

Rye Dale

Scawton Moor

White Horse

Wass Moor

Sproxton

A 168

Kilburn

Wass

Byland Abbey

Oswaldkirk

B1257

Ampleforth

R. Rye

A 19

Carlton Husthwaite

Coxwold

Howardian Hills

Gilling East

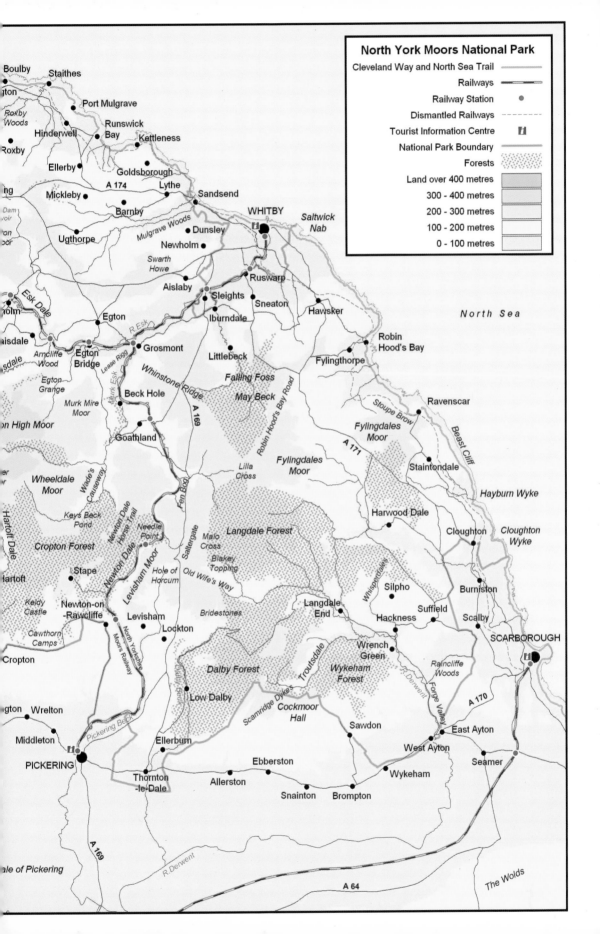

BILSDALE
and
THE WEST

The western boundary of the North York Moors is marked by one of the most spectacular escarpments in England. From Kilburn in the south to the Cleveland Hills in the north, a huge inland cliff divides the low-lying Vale of Mowbray from the high ground of the moors. The Cleveland Way National Trail follows the bank top, giving wonderful views to walkers.

A few miles east, the stunning valley of Bilsdale (left) cuts through the high moorland, effectively slicing the landscape in two.

This area has a series of delightful villages as well as the remains of great monastic houses at Rievaulx, Byland and Mount Grace Priory.

© Crown copyright and database rights 2012 Ordnance Survey 100021930

Sutton Bank and the western edge

The western escarpment, running from Kilburn to the Cleveland Hills, provides a succession of splendid views across the Vale of Mowbray, and the climb up Sutton Bank is a welcome sign that you are entering a different kind of landscape. Turn north along the bank and the rolling Hambleton Hills give way to forests and high moors before the edge of the plateau swings east to give views over the lower Tees Valley. Settlements on the margin of the plateau are few and far between, but down below there is a string of delightful villages, and the remains of Mount Grace Priory.

Sutton Bank

The North York Moors is an area of upland that stands above the surrounding country. The contrast between upland and lowland is magnificently shown on the western edge, where a steep, and sometimes vertical, escarpment marks the boundary.

The uplands once stretched further inland, but in the last ice age, a great ice sheet gouged out a flat-bottomed valley between the moors and the Pennines and formed the cliff at Sutton Bank. At the top of the bank you are standing

ABOVE: Great Spotted Woodpecker BELOW: Gormire Lake sits below Sutton Bank

on the edge of the old ice sheet. Hidden in the trees nearby is the National Park Centre. It is an essential stopping place for information of all kinds; and there is a tea room! Discover the geology of Sutton Bank in the Lime and Ice exhibition.

Gormire Lake

On the valley floor ice sheets made a dip in the ground and left meltwater behind to fill it. You can walk to Gormire Lake from the National Park Centre at Sutton Bank, through woodlands that are remnants of the native woods that once covered the moors. Birch and oak provide habitat for a good variety of woodland birds and insects.

Osmotherley Cross

Roulston Scar

The plateau just south of Sutton Bank is used by the Yorkshire gliding club, but is also the site of a massive hillfort built in the Iron Age, around 400 BC. The hillfort, the largest in the north of England, covered more than 24 hectares and some of the defences are still more than 2.5 metres in height.

Osmotherley

While this picturesque village dates back to Saxon times, Osmotherley developed into a small town in the early 19th century, to house workers in the quarries and textile industries. The market cross and a low, stone table stand on the green, and St Stephen's church, though restored in

Mount Grace Priory

Victorian times, has plenty of features from the 11th to 16th centuries.

Church at Over Silton

Mount Grace Priory

Set in woodland north of Osmotherley, the 14th century Mount Grace Priory is one of only ten Carthusian Priories founded in this country and is the best preserved. The monks lived solitary lives, one to a cell, with little contact between them.

Visitors can view a reconstructed monk's cell, a herb garden and an exhibition centre.

Remodelled in the early 20th century, the gardens are a haven for wildlife including the famous 'Priory Stoats'.

The high moors are crossed by a series of ancient tracks and roads, many of which have been preserved. They were used for all kinds of traffic, including packhorses and cattle driving, and some date back to prehistoric times. The most notable of the north-south routes is Hambleton Street, referred to in medieval documents as Regalis Via or King's Way, which is part of a route linking Yarm, Malton and York. Once carriages started using these roads in the 18th century, the gentry found them a little uncomfortable. The descent from Black Hambleton into Osmotherley was described in these terms in 1771: *'The going down into Cleveland is beyond all description, terrible, you go through such steep rough, narrow, rock precipices, that I would advise you to go a hundred miles to escape it.'*

Hambleton Street takes you past other historic features, such as Steeple Cross, a long barrow where five burials were found, Kepwick dikes, and old quarries and limekilns.

OUT AND ABOUT (*Titles of leaflets are in italics*)

 Walks around Sutton Bank, Six of the Best: Sutton Bank to Boltby; Cleveland Way National Trail.

 Cleveland Way north of Sneck Yate; Cold Kirby north to Hawnby and beyond; Hambleton Street.

 Bike Tracks; White Rose Cycle Route passes through Sutton Bank National Park Centre.

 Easy Going: Sutton Bank and the White Horse.

 Lime and Ice app for iPhone and iPod (available online)

WHERE ELSE CAN I SEE...

Ancient roads
The north-south roadways include the Via Magna running due north from Helmsley over Roppa edge, tracks following Bransdale and Rudland Riggs, the Blakey road and its daughter tracks, including the Quakers Causeway and the route to Guisborough Priory.

Monasteries
Ruins at Rievaulx and Byland; evidence of monastic houses at Baysdale, Lastingham, Hackness and Rosedale. Magnificent ruins at Whitby Abbey, Kirkham Abbey and Guisborough Priory lie just outside the National Park.

Roseberry Topping and the north west moors

The northwest edge of the National Park is marked by the magnificent sweep of the Cleveland Hills. Seen from below they are an imposing sight, dominating the skyline of the lower Tees valley; from above they offer views stretching as far as County Durham and the Pennines. These hills were once a valuable source of minerals, with alum, jet and ironstone all mined here. Even Roseberry Topping, Cleveland's most famous landmark, owes its shape to a major landslip caused by undermining.

Cleveland Hills

The highest point in the National Park is at Round Hill on Urra Moor, 454 metres above sea level. The summits of the Cleveland Hills stand above the surrounding country because they are made of hard sandstones sitting on top of soft shales.

Most of the North York Moors has hard Middle Jurassic rocks just below the surface, but where these have been cut through, by the sea or streams or ice, then Lower Jurassic rocks are exposed at the surface – and these are rich in minerals. The north face

of the Cleveland Hills was extensively mined, and the ironstone mines of East Cleveland were for decades the most productive in Britain. The scars of the mining industries

Urra Moor

remain and add to the fascination of these atmospheric hills.

Roseberry Topping

The splendid cone of Roseberry Topping stands in glorious isolation as an outlier of the Cleveland Hills. The shape of this famous landmark was dramatically altered in 1912 when old mineshafts on the south side collapsed, causing the side of the hill to fall away.

Roseberry Topping is held in great affection by the people of Cleveland, and everyone must climb to the summit at least once, where the 360 degree views are breathtaking.

Just north of here Guisborough Forest and Walkway give you a chance to see woodland and pond life, including newts, kingfishers and waxwings.

MOORLAND BIRDS

The high moorlands provide nesting grounds for five bird species that are worth looking out for. The merlin (below) is the smallest British bird of prey; you might catch a glimpse of it twisting and turning in flight. The red grouse is the prime resident of the moors, flying up suddenly when disturbed. The other three – curlew (above, with nestling), lapwing and golden plover – are waders, arriving on the moorland in the early part of the year. These are glorious birds with fluty calls and extravagant flight displays.

Curlew and lapwing also occur around the margins of the National Park. Most of the moorland is designated as a Special Protection Area, to help ground-nesting birds to thrive.

Railways and barrows

Battersby Junction is now a stop on the Esk Valley railway

Golden Plover

line – and a good starting point for exploring the National Park by train. But in the past, four lines met at Battersby, including the extraordinary railway that brought ironstone over the moors from Rosedale. The track of this line is still there, and the old drovers' road along Rudland Rigg also drops down from the moors near here, at Ingleby Bank. A group of four Bronze Age round barrows was excavated at Burton Howe revealing burials and cremations.

The Wain Stones on Hasty Bank

Baysdale Abbey

There was a Cistercian priory in the remote valley of Baysdale from around 1189. Twelve nuns and a prioress lived here, with continual reports of unsuitable prioresses and disreputable behaviour among the nuns! Nothing remains of the original priory buildings, though the Abbey Bridge, dating from the 13th century, carries the entrance to the Abbey over Grain Beck. The present farmhouse, known as Baysdale Abbey, dates mainly from the early 19th century.

Roseberry Topping
BELOW: *Captain Cook*

Captain Cook Monument

James Cook was born at Marton in 1728 and spent his childhood in Great Ayton, before working at Staithes and then Whitby. Cook's expeditions made him world famous, and he is acknowledged as the finest sea captain and navigator Britain has ever produced. A simple monument to Cook stands on a high point of Easby Moor overlooking Great Ayton.

OUT AND ABOUT

 Six of the Best: Sutton Bank to Boltby; walks from Guisborough Forest and Walkway Visitor Centre at Pinchinthorpe.

 Circular bridleway around Baysdale.

 Moor to Sea Cycle Route Network; Rudland Rigg to Ingleby Bank.

WHERE ELSE CAN I SEE...

Moorland wildlife
You are likely to come across wildlife anywhere on the moors, dales, forests and coast. See the National Park website for suggestions.

Outliers
Isolated hills like Roseberry Topping are outliers, left by erosion of the surrounding land. There are other notable outliers at Freeborough Hill near Lockwood Beck, Blakey Topping and Howden Hill, Langdale.

Bilsdale and Rievaulx

The western part of the North York Moors is sliced in two by the long valley of Bilsdale and Rye Dale. Cut by the River Seph, Bilsdale winds its way down from its high point at Hasty Bank, with stunning views over Cleveland, to join the Rye at Newgate, flowing south past Rievaulx and Helmsley. Renowned for its beauty, this area is full of fascinating historical sites, including Rievaulx Abbey and Spout House, as well as prehistoric remains on the high moors. And tucked away on the west side of Bilsdale are the hidden delights of Hawnby and the valley of the upper Rye.

Bilsdale

Rye Dale and Bilsdale have served as a route across the moors for centuries, but there are plenty of reasons to stop and explore this area. Erosion of the high moorland has created a series of spectacular outliers at Ashberry, Easterside, Coomb and Hawnby Hills. There is some beautiful walking country on the high moors, on Newgate Bank, Hasty Bank, in Bilsdale, and in upper Rye Dale and Ladhill Gill.

What's in a name?

The village of Chop Gate near the top of Bilsdale is sometimes pronounced 'Chop Yat'. 'Chop' comes from an Old Norse word 'ceap' or 'kaup' for chapman or pedlar. 'Yat' is local dialect for gate, which is the Norse word for a street or road. So Chop Gate means 'pedlars' way'.

Spout House

Spout House

A few miles south of Chop Gate, this remarkably well preserved 16th century, thatched cruck-framed house was once the local inn and centre of Bilsdale life. It closed in 1914 when the new Sun Inn was built. In 1982 the National Park Authority took over its care – it is now open to the public from Easter to October. This is a rare opportunity to see the inside of a cruck cottage, and sample the flavour of old rural life.

Ancient woodlands

To the east of Rievaulx, there are a series of ancient woodlands. Ashberry, Reins and Spring woods contain a mixture of birch, hazel, elm, alder and oak. Evidence of coppicing shows how these woods were used as a resource (see also page 42).

Hawnby and Rye Dale

From upper Hawnby there are fine views of the surrounding hillsides and into the valley of the Rye. A short distance from lower Hawnby is the parish church, set in solitude close to the River Rye. Nearby is the 17th century Arden Hall.

The villages are the gateway to the wooded valley of upper Rye Dale, with routes over the moors to Boltby and Osmotherley. To the north Snilesworth Moor has a Bronze Age field system and standing stones that look prehistoric but are thought to be a fairly modern stack stand for holding winter fodder.

Rievaulx

The magnificent ruins of the medieval monastery of Rievaulx Abbey sit in a secluded part of Rye Dale. The abbey was founded in 1131, at a time

LEFT: Saxon brooch BELOW: Snilesworth Standing Stones

when French monasteries were setting up satellite houses in England. The monks were drawn to the Yorkshire countryside because of its seclusion, but ironically the monasteries made this an agriculturally rich area, and Rievaulx became the finest and largest Cistercian house in England.

As well as their own grounds, the monasteries had satellite farms, or granges, across Yorkshire, and their level of organisation made them efficient at all kinds of farming and craft industries. The monks of Rievaulx had a large woolhouse and iron furnace at Laskill Farm.

Much of what was built by the monks at Rievaulx is in ruins today but a majority of the 13th century presbytery stands virtually to its full height. On the hilltop is Rievaulx Terrace and Temples, erected in 1758.

Rievaulx Ionic Temple

Old Byland and Scawton

Waves of incomers left traces (including a beautiful Anglo-Saxon brooch) and the churches of the area are good sites for historical detective work. Old Byland church has early Norman fragments and Scawton has one of the best preserved medieval village churches in England.

Rievaulx Abbey

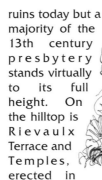

LIMESTONE GRASSLANDS

On the Tabular and Hambleton Hills the soils are naturally rich in calcium, derived from the limestone bedrock. Much of this country is good agricultural land, growing arable crops and productive leys (seeded grasslands). But unimproved limestone pastures and marginal areas produce wonderful arrays of wild flowers. Old quarries and the verges of forest tracks reveal cowslips in spring, milkwort and rock-rose in summer, and harebells and autumn gentian in August and September. Lime-loving plants like greater knapweed, salad burnet, fairy flax, marjoram, dogwood, violet and agrimony are also found here, as well as a wide variety of butterflies, in particular the pretty common blue.

OUT AND ABOUT

 Six of the Best: Hambleton Drove Road to Osmotherley; Helmsley to Rievaulx Waymark Walk; Snilesworth Moor.

 Fangdale Beck to Hawnby and Rievaulx.

 Bike Tracks: Routes Two, Three, Four and Six.

WHERE ELSE CAN I SEE...

Grassland flora
Around a quarter of the National Park is pasture; there are acid grasslands in the upper dales, supporting tormentil, bedstraw and bilberry, and neutral pastures in the lower dales with buttercups and purple betony among a host of other flowers.

Helmsley and the south

Tucked away below the wooded south-facing slopes of the Hambleton Hills is a string of lovely villages with fascinating connections, ranging from the author of Tristram Shandy to the mouseman of Kilburn and Oliver Cromwell's headless corpse! Here too are the magnificent ruins of Byland Abbey, and the unmissable White Horse. And as well as all that, there is the very special market town of Helmsley.

Helmsley

A picturesque market town on the banks of the River Rye, Helmsley has a fine spacious market square, dominated by an ancient market cross. The buildings around the square date from as early as the 16th century, and many of the shops make their own produce, including bread, cakes, chocolate and ice cream.

Helmsley Castle, which overlooks the town, has spectacular earthworks surrounding a great ruined keep. A well-preserved range of Eliza-bethan domestic buildings contain exhibitions.

Helmsley Walled Garden is gradually being restored to its former glory, including an orchid house. Plants, herbs, vegetables and fruit are grown and sold here.

Duncombe Park

The house in Duncombe Park, on the edge of Helmsley, was built in 1713, and is surrounded by 182 hectares of stunning parkland. There are views across Helmsley from the landscaped 18th century terraces, complete with temples, conservatory and secret 'scented garden'. A large portion of the grounds is a National Nature Reserve and home to ancient trees and many rare species of fungi and insects. Tree holes provide nest and roost sites for birds and bats, including kingfisher,

RIGHT: Nuthatch
BELOW: Duncombe Park with Helmsley Castle in background

grey wagtail and dipper along the river, and lesser-spotted woodpecker, nuthatch and hawfinch in the woodland.

Byland Abbey

The spectacular ruins of this ancient monastic house stand beneath the beautiful Hambleton Hills. A group of monks left Furness Abbey in Cumbria in 1134 and, after many years of wandering, and several false starts, moved to the site at Byland in 1177. By then many of the buildings were ready and the enormous

Rose window, Byland Abbey

church (as large as many cathedrals) was finished in the 1190s. Surviving features include elaborate mosaic tiles and the frame of the great rose window. You can also explore the remains of fishponds, dams and lakes built to drain the marshy land on which the abbey was built.

Ampleforth

A Benedictine monastery was founded here in an existing building in 1802. A church, monastery and school were added in the 19th and early 20th centuries, and Ampleforth Abbey and College is now a famous Catholic school.

ABOVE: Laurence Sterne
BELOW: The White Horse, Kilburn

Coxwold

Dominating the village is the octagonal tower of the 15th century parish church. Grassy banks with stone houses and cottages line the steep main street and there are several 17th century houses in the village.

Shandy Hall is named for Tristram Shandy, creation of Laurence Sterne, who was vicar of Coxwold and lived here from 1760 to his death in 1768. Sterne was one of the most celebrated writers of his day, and his works are recognised as milestones in world literature. His grave is in the churchyard.

Just south of Coxwold is Newburgh Priory, founded in the 12th century. The priory was later converted into a country mansion. The headless corpse of Oliver Cromwell is said to have been brought here in secret.

White Horse

This 70 metre high figure on the hillside above Kilburn was cut in 1857 by the residents of the village. It is unique in the north of England.

THE MOUSEMAN

People all over Yorkshire are familiar with the work of Robert Thompson. His beautifully made oak furniture always bore his distinctive 'signature', a small mouse, earning him the nickname The Mouseman of Kilburn. His work is now carried on in the village workshop in Kilburn which is run by Thompson's descendants. Each craftsman working there has a different mouse signature. The Mouseman showroom and visitor centre are open to the public.

There are lots of other craftspeople working in the region, including spinners, weavers, glass makers, potters and jewellers. See the local produce guide on the National Park website (see page 62).

OUT AND ABOUT

 Ampleforth Ancient Boundaries Walk. Oldstead, Roulston Scar and the White Horse of Kilburn; Oldstead, Byland Abbey and Mount Snever; Hambleton Monk's Way; Ampleforth Abbey Round.

 Cowhouse Bank to Riccal Bridge, Claythwaite Rigg.

 Sproxton to Wass, Byland and Oldstead.

WHERE ELSE CAN I SEE...

Nature Reserves
Forge Valley (page 58) is a National Nature Reserve, recognised by Natural England as being of national importance. The Bridestones in Dalby Forest, Garbutt Wood, Scaling Dam and Hayburn Wyke are among the other reserves run by the National Trust, Northumbrian Water and the Yorkshire Wildlife Trust.

19

ESK DALE
and the
NORTH WEST

The north of the National Park is dominated by the valley of the Esk, the dales of its tributaries, and the moors that lie above. The combination of high moorland, dales full of pasture fields, and beautiful streams and rivers provides a captivating landscape. The Esk itself is a haven for wildlife, including salmon, sea trout, otters and kingfishers. In Esk Dale, Danby Dale, Glaisdale and elsewhere, you can discover fascinating buildings, historic bridges and a succession of picturesque villages. Just beneath the surface is an intriguing industrial history, complete with mines, quarries and ironworks. All of this can be reached via the Esk Valley Railway, one of the most delightful railway lines in Britain.

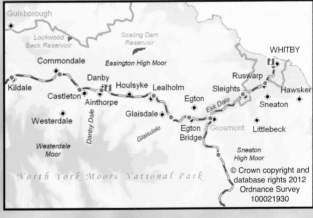

© Crown copyright and database rights 2012 Ordnance Survey 100021930

Westerdale to Castleton

The River Esk rises in Westerdale, above Esklets crag, and flows north before turning east above Castleton and flowing on to Whitby. The Esk shows its own peculiar history by behaving like a mature river with a wide flood plain and meandering course in its upper portion, and then tumbling like a young stream once it gets past Lealholm. The dales around the upper Esk are lovely tranquil places, while Castleton is a busy working village.

ABOVE: Westerdale ABOVE RIGHT: Dipper RIGHT: Kingfisher

Esk Lake

During the last Ice Age the upper Esk valley was submerged beneath a lake. A lobe of ice pushed up the valley from the sea, forming a dam above present-day Lealholm and pushing the surface of the lake as high as the dale tops. The upper Esk winds its way across an old lake bed before dropping into a narrow valley below Glaisdale.

Bridging the Esk

The 20 or so bridges that cross the Esk between Westerdale and Whitby are a fascinating subject in themselves (the National Park Authority has a leaflet called *Bridges of the Esk*). The first, known as Hunters Sty, is at the bottom of Westerdale village. Restored in 1874, it may date from the 13th century. Two kilometres downstream is Dibble Bridge

(dibble means a deep pool), a double arch first recorded in 1301. These are extraordinary pieces of history, surviving from a time when monks and other medieval travellers began to move goods and animals across the moors; a sign that agriculture and trade were becoming more organised.

Hunters Sty bridge

High dales and moors

Due to the underlying rock, the dales north of the Esk are less extensive than those to the south. Tranquil Commondale was an industrial site in the 19th century, with limekilns and a large-scale brickworks. The moors above have ancient paved tracks or trods, and the Quaker's Causeway crosses Stanghow Moor to the north, en route to Guisborough Priory.

To the south, Westerdale is a classic landform – a winding, steep-sided, flat-bottomed dale, with springs and becks pouring into it from all sides. The head waters of the Esk have exposed the bedrock at Esklets Crag. Notice how the dale head slots between the heads of Rosedale and Farndale like the fingers of two hands.

Trod, Commondale

Castleton

The village is unusual for the moors, with its winding main street having an almost continuous terrace of houses on either side. The reason is the late flourishing of the village, which was still a tiny hamlet in the late 18th century, before becoming the main market town and industrial focus of the upper Esk valley.

The village is built on the edge of the steep hillside overlooking Eskdale and was, as the name suggests, the site of a medieval castle, sited on

Castle Hill. Castleton grew as a market town, with annual cattle, wool and cheese fairs. There was also a silk mill here and the parish church has furniture by Robert Thompson of Kilburn.

Otter

The uplands began to be settled by hunter-foragers from around 6000 BC. Later Bronze Age settlers gradually felled the forests, built barrows to bury their leaders, cleared the land by piling stones into cairns and began to make field boundaries. From about 1,000 BC they built great dyke systems to divide the land.

The upland soils became impoverished and a cooler, wetter climate stimulated growth of a thick layer of peat. The moorland was abandoned, allowing an astonishing amount of prehistoric material to survive.

There are more than 200 barrows, or howes, on the moors, including Western Howes and Pike Howe and Three Howes above Castleton. Food vessels, incense cups, bone pins and a stone battleaxe have been found here, while flint arrow heads are found across the moors. Other howes contained burial urns.

Remains of around 70 Bronze Age farms, with cairnfields and boundaries, have been discovered. At Crown End in Westerdale an Iron Age enclosure may indicate a change from crops to pastoral farming.

OUT AND ABOUT

 The Esk Valley Walk runs from Westerdale Moor to Whitby; *Walks in the Esk Valley* (online).

 Quaker's Causeway bridleway across Stanghow Moor.

 Moor to Sea Cycle Network from Great Ayton to Whitby goes through Commondale and Castleton.

WHERE ELSE CAN I SEE...

Bronze Age remains
Most of the high moors have Bronze Age remains such as cairnfields, barrows or field systems; see also local museums.

Danby to Lealholm

The series of dales dipping down from the high moors into the valley of the Esk continues with Danby Dale, Little Fryup and Great Fryup Dale. On the north side, Esk Dale rises steeply to Danby Beacon and the high plateau of Easington High Moor and on to Scaling Dam. The dales are populated with scattered farms (with the notable exception of Botton village) with the villages of Ainthorpe, Danby, Houlsyke and Lealholm nestled close to the Esk. Here too is The Moors National Park Centre, a mine of information and a good starting point for exploring the area.

Primroses

Danby and Ainthorpe

The neighbouring villages of Ainthorpe and Danby are on opposite sides of the Esk. Ainthorpe boasts the oldest pub in the area, the Fox and Hounds, which dates back to 1555. Danby was once the home of Canon Atkinson, author of *Forty Years In A Moorland Parish*, an idealised account of life on the moors in the 19th century.

The cottages in many of these villages were built for estate workers, including those engaged in industrial trades such as coal and iron-

Danby Castle

stone mining. Danby shops sell local produce, including bread and cakes. The area around the villages is also full of interest. Esk Mill is a restored water mill, the medieval Duck Bridge (built in 1396, and restored in 1717), is nearby and Danby Church is some distance from the village, in a beautiful location up the dale.

The Moors National Park Centre and Crow Wood

Danby Lodge was a fashionable shooting lodge in the 18th century. Today it is the Moors National Park Centre, with information, shop, exhibitions, gallery and café. The lovely grounds contain a children's play area. Crow Wood contains remnants of the wood that covered most of Esk Dale until 2000 years ago. Much of this wood has been cleared for farmland but one or two ancient oaks remain. A variety of ornamental trees were

The Moors National Park Centre

planted in the mid 19th century. A bird hide and feeding station allow you to see a variety of woodland birds, including goldfinch and nuthatch.

Danby Castle

One of the most interesting buildings in the region, Danby Castle dates from the early 1300s.

Built for Lord Latimer, the castle was once the home of Catherine Parr, sixth wife of Henry VIII. It was a pioneering architectural design, combining defence with comfortable living, and providing a model for later fortified houses. The castle is now a working farm, with part of the original building used as a farmhouse. Danby Court Leet, an ancient body that administers common land and other matters, meets in the Castle's courtroom. Of 12 courts leet surviving in England, three are on the North York Moors.

Locally-made bread and cakes in Danby

Danby Beacon

At 299 metres Danby Beacon is a superb viewpoint over the Esk Valley. The moors to the north carry plenty of traces of prehistoric use and are crossed by ancient tracks, including the Pannierman's Causeway. The small valley of Clitherbeck, north of Danby village is littered with disused coal shafts and waste heaps.

Lealholm

Steep hillsides lead down to Lealholm village green which slopes down to the riverside, alongside the one-arched bridge. The Poet's Cottage Shrub Nursery is named after John Castillo, a local poet, stonemason and preacher who lived there in the 19th century.

Lealholm bridge

FARMING THE DALES

Danby Show

The sharp divide between heather moorland and green dales shows up clearly in Danby Dale and the Fryup Dales. The dales have been farmed for thousands of years, but agriculture became highly organised in late medieval times. Great estates were given to Norman knights, and parts of these were granted to monasteries. Tenant farmers kept sheep and cattle in the dales and laid out field boundaries we see today. The uplands were kept for hunting by the lords, and houses with names like Grange Head Farm and Hall Grange Farm near Egton were estate houses, while Butter Park was one of several deer parks.

In the 18th century, the age of land enclosures, attempts were made to colonise more of the moorland for pasture, but these were only marginally successful. The improvements in agriculture did bring benefits to some; Fryup Hall is an early example of a substantial house built for a prosperous farmer, rather than a member of the nobility.

Farming today often follows old-established patterns, with tough Swaledale sheep put onto the moors, and then brought in for lambing, and cattle kept further down.

The country shows held in the summer, including Danby show, are an unmissable chance to sample the enduring customs and atmosphere of rural life.

Botton Village

High up in Danby Dale this village is run by the Camphill Trust. Adults with special needs live in community houses. The public are welcome to visit the various workshops and coffee shop.

OUT AND ABOUT

 The Esk Valley Walk; *Walks from The Moors Centre*; through and around Danby Dale and the Fryup Dales, and on the moors to the north.

 Danby Beacon to Lealholm Rigg; bridleways on Ainthorpe, Danby and Glaisdale Riggs.

 Moor to Sea Cycle Network to Danby Beacon and on to Egton.

 Easy Going: Crow Wood at The Moors National Park Centre (online).

WHERE ELSE CAN I SEE...

Country shows

There are shows at Sneaton, Egton, Hinderwell, Osmotherley, Thornton-le-Dale, Rosedale, Farndale, Kildale, Castleton and elsewhere. See annual guides and websites for details.

Glaisdale to Aislaby

The villages of Esk Dale each have their own story, but there is a common history. There were small hamlets near crossing points over the river, as at lower Glaisdale and Egton Bridge, or part way up the daleside, as at upper Glaisdale, Egton and Aislaby. But when mining and rail travel got going in the nineteenth century, the Esk villages expanded hugely. A village was built at Grosmont and remote Goathland became a tourist site (see page 52). The remnants of Esk Dale's industrial boom – stone cottages and disused quarries – are now a picturesque part of the landscape. The dales at Glaisdale and the Murk Esk have fascinating remnants of even older history.

ABOVE: River Esk
BELOW: Witch post

Glaisdale

The village of Glaisdale is spread along a road that winds up from the river and along the southern side of Esk Dale. Terraces were built in the 19th century to accommodate ironstone workers, and down below is the Beggar's Bridge, the most famous of all the Esk crossings. Legend has it that one Thomas Ferries had to wade across the Esk to court his lover, whose father thought him too poor. Ferries went away to make his fortune (he became a sea captain and fought against the Armada) and returned to marry his sweetheart. He built the bridge, in 1619, so that others would not have the same trouble. Though it carries the date 1619, the Beggar's Bridge is a medieval packhorse bridge, so it may have been rebuilt by Ferries.

Shops in Glaisdale and elsewhere in Esk Dale and the moors are well-known for their local produce.

Bronze age jet necklace and bronze spearhead

Woods and witches

In this area the Esk valley is richly wooded, with the beautiful Arncliff woods spreading along the Esk and up through Glaisdale. Mixed broadleaf and coniferous woods stretch up to the dale head.

Many farmhouses in this area had rowan wood posts, carved with X-shaped patterns at each side of the hearth. These were witch posts, designed to stop witches gaining entry. Postgate Farm in Glaisdale, which dates from 1664, has two witch posts, as does Quarry Farm. Right up at the head of the dale is Witch Hill.

Peat bogs

On Glaisdale Moor, Egton High Moor and elsewhere, peat depths can reach several metres deep, forming dangerous peat bogs in places. But the peat is fragile and erosion by over-use or destruction by fire can be devastating. The route of the Lyke Wake Walk from Osmotherley

Pork pies, made and sold locally

INDUSTRY

It might be hard to believe but tranquil Esk Dale was, in the 19th century, an industrial valley. Alum, coal, ironstone and whinstone were mined in the dales, and iron, bricks and setts were manufactured in the villages. Industry changed the face of the area, with mines, quarries and huge iron works dominating the landscape. Drift mines were dug into the dalesides at different levels making a honeycomb of subterranean tunnels and workings.

The vast growth of Victorian Britain pro-duced demand for everything including paving stone. The Cleveland Dyke, a vertical slab of hard volcanic rock (known as whinstone) that runs across Esk Dale near Egton Bridge, was quarried for setts to pave the streets of Victorian Leeds.

Most of the cottages in Esk Dale were built for industrial workers. Aislaby is typical of many villages – Woodlands is a grand house built from alum industry profits, while White Row terrace was built for quarrymen.

Egton Bridge

Egton Bridge is the site of the 200-year-old Gooseberry Show. Held in August, the biggest entries weigh in at around 32 drams, about the size of a golf ball!

Grosmont

When workmen dug cuttings for the railway in the 1830s, they discovered high-grade ironstone, and Grosmont became a boom town. Iron ore was shipped out by rail and, when the boom evaporated in the 1890s, the railway took local people to Liverpool to emigrate to the New World.

Egton Bridge

A fine stone bridge was rebuilt here in 1992 in the style of the original, which was washed away by floods in the 1930s.

to Ravenscar has been varied to prevent erosion of the moorland peat. Egton Moor has also yielded prehistoric remains, such as the Bronze Age jet necklace and spearhead shown here.

Egton

The village of Egton stands at a crossroads on level ground, high above Esk Dale. Each August Egton hosts one of the largest agricultural shows in the region. Egton was the home of the Blessed Nicholas Postgate, the Roman Catholic martyr hanged for his faith at York in 1679. St Hedda's Catholic Church has a shrine to the martyr.

OUT AND ABOUT

 Numerous walks in this area including Glaisdale, Murk Mire Moor, Egton to Westonby. *Walks in the Esk Valley* (online).

 Glaisdale Moor to Wain Hill, bridleway from near Egton Bridge up to Murk Mire Moor, *Newtondale Horse Trail*.

 Moor to Sea Cycle Network along minor roads from Glaisdale to Aislaby.

WHERE ELSE CAN I SEE...

Industrial remains
There are old quarries along Whinstone Ridge on Goathland Moor, iron workings at Rosedale, and alum quarries and works along Carlton Bank, at Boulby, Kettleness, Sandsend and Ravenscar.

Sleights to Sneaton

The steep-sided valley of Iburndale carries May Beck and Little Beck from the heights of Fylingdales Moor down to the Esk below Sleights. On the way the waters tumble over Falling Foss and pass the tiny village of Littlebeck. Further down the Esk is the lovely riverside village of Ruswarp and, to the east, the open country around Sneaton. Tucked away from the main through routes, this is a delightful corner of the National Park.

ABOVE: Boating at Ruswarp
RIGHT: Pied Flycatcher

Sleights

Built on the south side of Esk Dale, Sleights was favoured by successful traders and seamen from Whitby. Handsome houses, such as Carr Hill, Esk Hall and the Old Vicarage were built for gentry and merchants on the long, steep hill that descends to the bridge

May Beck

over the heavily-wooded banks of the Esk. On Sleights Moor there is a large round barrow and the remains of two stone circles.

East of Sleights is the village of Ugglebarnby, whose curious name is derived from the Scandinavian nickname of 'Owlbeard'. The 19th-century church contains a font, pulpit and reredos of elaborately carved stone.

Ruswarp

The former mill, now converted into flats, is a dominant feature of the riverside at Ruswarp. It was originally built in 1752 but was burnt out in 1911. After rebuilding, the mill continued working until 1989. While most bridges further up the Esk are stone-built, Ruswarp bridge shows how technology changes – built in 1936, it is made of steel manufactured at Dorman Long in Middlesbrough. The village is at the tidal limit of the river;

hire a boat here and you can row from the weir up to the bridge at Sleights.

The last section of the Esk Valley Walk takes you on from Ruswarp to Whitby. This is a great way to enter Whitby, with the town and harbour emerging as you walk along the river side.

Sneaton

The village of Sneaton enjoys views across the hillside towards the River Esk and the sea at Whitby. The hilltop here was used for a warning beacon during the threat from the Spanish Armada. St Hilda's church in Sneaton has a wonderful new stained glass window depicting Caedmon, the first English poet, by Lythe artist Alan Davie. The window was commissioned in 2000 to mark the millennium.

Iburndale and Littlebeck

The valley of Iburndale is, like many stretches of the lower Esk, narrow and steep-sided. When the Esk Dale ice sheet retreated, the streams that drained the surrounding moors cut deep gorges through the glacial mud that was left behind.

Narrow lanes, sharp bends and extreme gradients mark the route to the small settlement of Littlebeck.

Like most riverside hamlets,

Caedmon window, Sneaton

FALLING FOSS

Up on the dale heads across the North York Moors you will sometimes come across small waterfalls. Waterfalls are made by streams tumbling over hard slabs onto soft rocks below. On the moors these waterfalls mark the boundary between the hard sandstone of the moorland, and the softer shales beneath that line the dales.

High waterfalls are rare in this area, the most spectacular exception being Falling Foss, a mile or so south of Littlebeck in Iburndale. Here, in a beautiful wooded valley, May Beck slides over a slab of hard sandstone and falls more than 9 metres. After heavy rain the waterfall is a particularly stirring sight.

The upper part of the dale has lovely woodland walks following the May Beck and Little Beck streams. In spring and summer, wildflowers blanket the floor and there is a wealth of birdlife including redstarts, pied flycatchers, wood-warblers and green woodpeckers.

the village had a watermill, now a cottage.

Pools and lakes

The waters of the valley have been exploited in other ways. Just south of the village there are the remains of an open air concrete swimming pool and small boating lake. The bathing pool was opened around 1934 but by 1945 was a swamp containing a vast number of frogs! The boating lake has reverted to a bog full of trees and bullrushes.

On Parsley Beck, further up the dale, a local landowner blocked the stream with two large iron doors to form a lake stocked with fish. Now returned to a semi-natural state, it remains an interesting sight with an island in the middle and dense vegetation on the banks.

Moorland deceptions

Recent history has left traces in this area. Parts of Fylingdales Moor were used as firing ranges in the Second World War, and decoy fires were used to convince enemy bombers that targets on Teesside had already been hit. Old cartridge cases are still found, and remnants of brick and concrete bunkers are now embedded in the moorland.

Common frog

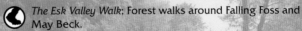

OUT AND ABOUT

The Esk Valley Walk; Forest walks around Falling Foss and May Beck.

Bridleways on Leas Head Road, Foster Howes Rigg, and Robin Hood's Bay Road.

Moor to Sea Cycle Network from Egton to Whitby; links to the old Whitby to Scarbrough railway at Ruswarp.

WHERE ELSE CAN I SEE...

Waterfalls
Mallyan Spout and Thomasson Foss, both near Goathland; small falls at head of Great Fryup Dale, on the Derwent in Langdale Forest.

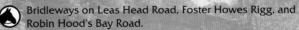

The HERITAGE COAST

From Boulby in the north to Cloughton in the south, the Heritage Coast is one of England's natural wonders. A series of towering cliffs, rocky inlets and sweeping bays give an unbroken coastline of breathtaking beauty. There are beaches and coves but this coast is loved mainly for its wild and untamed nature. Even the picturesque villages of the coast, like Robin Hood's Bay (left), seem to grow out of the natural landscape; tucked into the gulleys between the cliffs, they still provide welcome shelter and refreshment to travellers.

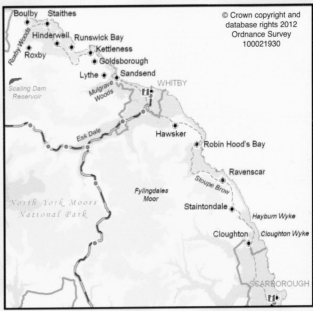

Staithes and the north east

The north east corner of the National Park sees great piles of Jurassic rocks meet the sea. The result is a series of breath-taking vertical cliffs – among the highest in England – with old fishing villages tucked into narrow gorges leading down to the sea. Staithes and Runswick are famously picturesque, as are the 200-metre-high tops of Boulby cliff. Inland there are the more tranquil pleasures of Hinderwell village, Roxby Woods and Scaling Dam Reservoir.

Yorkshire Coble

Staithes

The old village is known for its higgledy-piggledy streets with cottages, houses and chapels built virtually on top of each other, crammed into a narrow gap in the cliff. Dog Loup is the narrowest street in Yorkshire - you might need to turn sideways to get through it!

used for drying and curing fish. From the 1870s the railways took ironstone direct to Middlesbrough cutting out the coastal ports, while fresh fish went to the growing cities of the West Riding and Lancashire.

The boats used for fishing were the famous Staithes coble, a clinker-built boat made and used for inshore work all along the Yorkshire coast, with a large five-man boat used further out to sea. When trawlers arrived from elsewhere in the early 20th century, villagers continued to fish inshore, but others had to look for work on the land and in the mines.

The village began to extend up onto the cliff top from the 1870s, with further development in the 1930s and 1960s, though the village remained a self-contained community with its own distinctive customs, until recent times. The history of the village and its connections with Captain Cook, can be explored at the Heritage Centre.

Runswick

Like Staithes, Runswick devel-

Fulmar

oped as a sea access for cement and iron, while the villagers made a living from fishing. The sandy bay allowed easy landing of inshore boats and smuggling and shipwrecks also provided a steady income. Nowadays little fishing is done and the village is simply a beautiful place to live.

The wooded valleys that lead into the bay are notable for their wildflowers - blue-

Roaching casks for alum

Boulby alum cisterns

In the early 1800s Staithes was the largest fishing port on this coast, with ironstone passing through as well as thousands of tons of fish. The village was a hive of activity with every available space

Staithes can seem isolated today, but in its heyday local seamen were familiar with the oceans, ports and customs of the world, making it more cosmopolitan than inland towns. The railways brought other people to the village, including a series of landscape artists who became known as the Staithes Group. From around 1890 Laura Knight, Frederick Jackson, Charles Mackie,

'Hauling Cobles', Lionel Townsend Crawshaw

Rowland Hill and others followed the French impressionist fashion for founding artists' colonies and painting in the open air. They lived among the Staithes fishing community and held their first group exhibition in 1901. The group dispersed at the outbreak of war in 1914. Their work continued the strong and ongoing response of artists to the wild and shifting beauty of the moors and sea.

bells and violets, moschatel and lily-of-the-valley, as well as wood vetch and old man's beard.

Boulby and minerals

At Boulby a layer of hard sandstone sits on top of softer shales giving a series of vertical cliffs. Old alum quarries stretch north of Boulby Grange, with the remains of the alum works still preserved. Ironstone was mined in East Cleveland until the 1960s and shipped to Tyneside and the Tees. Access to the sea was via a jetty at Staithes, and the harbour at Port Mulgrave. Iron rails were laid across the scar for carts to carry ironstone to the pier at Staithes. All along the coast ruts (many still visible) were made in the scar to guide carts carrying minerals and kelp.

Runswick Bay

Nowadays Boulby is the site of a huge potash mine, bringing minerals from 1.5 kilometres beneath the ground.

Roxby and Scaling Dam

The woods at Roxby run inland along twin valleys originally created by glacial meltwater. Woodland animals and plants take advantage of this secluded spot. The site of Romano-British houses have been discovered at Roxby.

Just to the south, Scaling Dam reservoir has facilities for sailing and wind surfing. Part of the lake is a Nature Reserve with a hide for bird-watching. Species recorded here include goldeneye, teal, wigeon and little grebe.

OUT AND ABOUT

 Cleveland Way/North Sea Trail, including circular walk from Staithes to Hinderwell and Newton Mulgrave.

 Bridleways on Newton Mulgrave Moor, Roxby High Moor and Borrowby Moor.

WHERE ELSE CAN I SEE...

Artists' work
There are artists of all kinds, including painters, sculptors, potters and glass-makers, at work throughout the National Park, with galleries showing their work in many villages and towns in the area. The Pannett Art Gallery in Whitby has a fine display of work by Staithes Group artists. In the summer there is a series of Open Studios weekends.

Kettleness and Sandsend

From the spectacular headlands of Kettleness and Sandsend Ness, the land takes a sudden dive down to sea-level. Sandsend is one of the few places where the coast forgets its towering cliffs and windy headlands, and becomes a pleasant sandy beach. Kettleness is a wild majestic outpost and an unmissable viewpoint for the northern coast – even the Romans knew that. At the top of the cliff above Sandsend is the village of Lythe with its fascinating church and, tucked away in the valley down below, is Mulgrave Castle and surrounding woods.

Cliff top walks
A walk around the Kettleness headland gives wonderful views of Boulby and Runswick Bay, with the picturesque village in full view to the north, and of Sandsend and Whitby to the south.

In late winter the cliff-top fields have flocks of lapwings vying with gulls for feeding rights, and by early spring seabirds are starting to nest on ledges just below the cliff path.

Roman look outs
On the highest point of the headland, just north of Goldsborough, lie the remains of a Roman signal station dating from the fourth century AD. A string of stations along this coast were used as lookouts and warning beacons for attacks from the continent. Human remains found at Goldsborough suggest that the watchmen met a violent death.

A hoard of Roman coins discovered at Ugthorpe in 1998 is on display in Whitby Museum. The silver denarius was the main coin of the empire, equivalent to a day's pay for a soldier.

Plesiosaur

Lythe and Mulgrave
The site of the church at Lythe has been used for Christian worship for over 1,000 years. Rebuilt in 1910 with earlier portions incorporated, it has rare and precious pieces of Viking sculpture and gravestones. The old paved pannierways used by monks and traders are still visible on the footpaths running north from Lythe church. These were the highways of medieval England carrying foot traffic and pack animals.

Once the largest parish in the region, Lythe contained seven separate townships or settlements; the joining of

Kettleness

Lapwings

Suggested reconstruction of a Roman signal station

Ammonites with iron pyrites

these Saxon settlements in one parish reflected the granting of a vast estate to the De Mornay family by William the Conqueror.

The beautiful valley between Lythe and Sandsend is a private estate containing Mulgrave Castle and Mulgrave Woods. Access to the old castle (now a picturesque ruin) and to certain sections of this ancient woodland, is allowed on Wednesdays and weekends (closed in May). The twin valleys cut by Sandsend and East Row Becks were originally made by meltwater flowing around the edge of an ice lobe.

Gold ammonites

Look carefully on the flat scar at the north end of Sandsend beach and you might see small ammonites embedded in the rock. Some of these have been mineralised with iron pyrites – 'fool's gold' –

Lythe Church

and have the beautiful appearance of gold ornaments. They get exposed as the sea washes away the surrounding rock. If you find one, leave it for someone else to discover.

ALUM AND REPTILES

Below the cliff-top path at Kettleness is a peculiar landscape. The scooped out nose of the headland holds the remains of a huge alum quarry. Thousands of tons of alum shale were hacked out and processed, between 1650 and around 1870, leaving behind a vast area of grey shale, which even the hardiest plants struggle to colonise.

While digging, the Kettleness quarrymen unearthed a series of spectacular fossil reptiles – plesiosaurs and ichthyosaurs – as well as ammonites, belemnites and other fossil shells. The cliffs just north of Sandsend were also quarried for alum, jet and cement, and the row of neat cottages that runs up the beck was built for alum workers. Fossil reptiles are still being found at Kettleness and some spectacular specimens are on display in Whitby Museum.

OUT AND ABOUT

 Sandsend Trail; *Six of the Best: Lythe to Runswick Bay*; Cleveland Way/North Sea Trail.

 Bridleways in Hutton Mulgrave Wood; Sandsend Beach.

 Cycle the Coast: Lythe to Mickleby (online).

WHERE ELSE CAN I SEE...

Fossils

The Yorkshire coast is famous for its fossils but if you walk along the scars always check tide tables and don't go near the foot of cliffs – there are continual dangerous rock falls. Fossils are easiest to find in scattered loose material. Many of the shore-lines between Saltburn and Scarborough have fossils; in summer you can join organized fossil walks run by the Dinosaur Coast project and other providers. Visit Whitby and Scarborough Museums to see impressive fossil displays and learn more about geology.

Saltwick to Robin Hood's Bay

The towering cliffs that run south from Whitby and Saltwick provide thrilling views and wild scenery before dipping down to provide one of the most captivating sights on the coast. The great arc of Robin Hood's Bay, made by the sea's erosion of a huge dome of rock strata, is a stunning natural amphitheatre. The towering headlands to the north and south, the shelf below Stoupe Brow, the high moors just above, and the steep winding streets of the village all add to the charms of Robin Hood's Bay.

Fishermen c1900

Saltwick

In the cliffs and just above the water line, alum and jet were dug out of the rocks and out of the great mound of Saltwick Nab. This is a treacherous coast though, with rocky scars and tides that wash in to the foot of vertical cliff-faces.

Kittiwakes

Baytown

The village of Robin Hood's Bay – variously called Baytown or simply Bay – is one of the most beautiful in Britain. The houses are crammed into the narrow streets and built almost one on top of another. Before a sea wall was built in 1975 over 200 houses had been lost through cliff falls.

FYLINGDALES FIRE

In September 2003 a fire that started in a lay-by spread across a section of Fylingdales Moor, just west of Stoupe Brow. The fire burned for 3 to 4 days, devastating the heather and fragile peat soils. Within the burnt area were 30 Scheduled Monuments, including the impressive Robin Hood's Butts barrows, parts of a prehistoric field system and a scattering of rock art.

Detail of decoration from Late Neolithic (c. 2500 BC) decorated rock found on Fylingdales Moor

heather and peat was astonishing. Over 190 decorated rock art panels were recorded in an area of 2.5 sq km . This was far more than previously known, and included the 4,500-year-old stone seen here. Further examples of Bronze Age burial mounds were found, and remains from much later times, including water channels for the alum works, were also uncovered.

An extraordinary amount of undiscovered material was revealed by the destruction of the dense vegetation, and the peat. Bronze Age settlement of the moors was well-known, as were samples of rock art - mainly abstract patterns carved onto stones. But the density of remains found beneath the

Without its protective layer of peat and heather, the soil began to erode, damaging archaeological features. Six organisations combined to mount a huge operation to regenerate the vegetation. The heather is growing back and the archaeological sites, having been photographed and recorded, are becoming covered again.

Rock pools are teeming with life

Fishing was the main reason for the village's existence. In its heyday in the 1820s there were 35 cobles and five large herring boats working, with several hundred villagers involved in the industry. The coming of the railway in 1885 expanded the market to the whole country. But bigger boats were being used and the lack of a harbour brought on a decline in Bay's fishing. But inshore fish, including crabs and lobsters, are still sold locally.

Nearby Hawsker, Fylingthorpe and Stoupe Brow are linked by the track of the old railway, which gives stunning views across the bay.

Smuggling

The location and layout of Bay proved ideal for smuggling. In the 18th century barrels of brandy, chests of tea and bales of silk were brought from Holland and landed in secret. Many of the houses were connected by internal passageways, so contraband could be moved from the dock to the top of town without seeing the light of day. From there it went overland to Saltergate and beyond.

Smuggling provided a good living for many and only died out when duties on imports were reduced in the 1800s.

Rock pools

The shoreline is home to an array of fascinating living creatures. The mix of rocky and sandy shores, the rock pools and boulders hold a wide variety of shellfish, seaweeds of all kinds, anemones, shrimps, bristle worms, hermit crabs and starfish. Sea birds come to feed here, with red-legged oystercatchers patrolling the sea edge.

Fossils

At Robin Hood's Bay rocks of the Lower Jurassic period are exposed, with lots of fossils of belemnites and ammonites. If you want to collect fossils, pick them up from loose material in the gullies and rock pools. The bay is popular, but

there are plenty of other places to look – at Sandsend, Whitby and Saltwick, for example. Remember, if you wander away along any shore always check the tides, and avoid the bottom of steep cliffs; rock falls are common and very dangerous.

OUT AND ABOUT

 Walks Around Robin Hood's Bay; Six of the Best: Whitby to Hawsker; Cleveland Way/North Sea Trail.

 Old Scarborough to Whitby railway; bridleway on Howdale Moor.

 Cycle the Coast: Whitby to Hawsker and *Robin Hood's Bay (online);* Moor to Sea Cycle Network.

WHERE ELSE CAN I SEE...

Prehistoric remains

Round barrows at, for example, Three Howes Rigg (Castleton), Hob-on-the-Hill (Commondale), Lilla Howe (east of Goathland), Swarth Howe (near A171 north of Whitby). Archaeological finds from the moors are on display in Whitby, Scarborough, Malton and York museums.

Belemnite fossils

Ravenscar to Cloughton Wyke

South from the great headland at Ravenscar runs a series of high cliffs with access to the sea restricted to Hayburn Wyke, with its lovely wooded dale, and Cloughton Wyke. The North Sea Trail section of the Cleveland Way runs through here, having followed the coast all the way from Saltburn. The cliff top views – particularly south to Scarborough Castle – are spectacular, while inland there are the delightful hills and dales around Staintondale and the track of the old Scarborough to Whitby railway.

Alum

The alum works of the Yorkshire coast were one of England's earliest chemical industries and a vital part of the economy for centuries. Alum from here was used in cloth dyeing and leather tanning when woollen textiles were England's most important export.

The quarries and the remains of the works are best seen at Ravenscar. From the 1600s to the 1870s alum shale was quarried out before being roasted, leached and treated, until the pure alum crystals were produced.

The alum was taken down to the beach below the works, and along carriageways cut in the scar before being shipped up the coast. Hundreds of people worked in apparently remote places – but before the railways, the coastal waters were the highways of trade and industry.

Reconstruction of Peak Alum Works c.1850

Hayburn Wyke

Beast Cliff

All along this coast the high cliffs have seen occasional collapses and landslips. Sometimes these cause a lower level of cliff to form as a platform. One of the most interesting of these undercliffs is Beast Cliff, between Ravenscar and Hayburn. The variety of undisturbed habitats supports a distinctive flora including honeysuckle and fragrant orchids.

Long distance trails

The Cleveland Way, one of Britain's first National Trails, opened in 1969. It runs for 175 kilometres from Helmsley in a great horseshoe, taking in the northern moors and the coast, before finishing at Filey. The section from Saltburn

to Filey is part of the North Sea Trail, which offers walking opportunities on the coast in Britain and other North Sea countries.

The National Cycle Network is being continually developed and the old railway between Scarborough and Whitby is now open for use by walkers, riders and cyclists. In this section, the old railway runs through a lovely piece of farming country.

Hayburn Wyke

The small coastal inlets in this area are called wykes, from the Nordic word 'vic'. At Hayburn Wyke a beautiful wooded valley flanks the beck down to a boulder-strewn beach. The woods, now owned by the National Trust and managed as a Nature Reserve, have native species like ash, oak and hazel, and are a haven for birds such as redstart, blackcap and pied flycatcher. The old Scarborough to Whitby railway passes through Hayburn Wyke, which, with a handy hotel, made this a favourite outing in Victorian times.

Staintondale

The village at Staintondale is a collection of far-flung farmsteads. This is typical of Viking settlements, but the ending '-ton' is Anglo-Saxon, so it may have been a single settlement that was added to.

RAVENSCAR

The small settlement of Ravenscar stands on the mighty headland (created by a massive geological fault) at the south end of Robin Hood's Bay. From here the views over the bay are stunning, with walks along Stoupe Brow and down to the shore. Sea birds in this area include cormorants and fulmars.

Ravenscar is sometimes called 'the resort that never was'. In the 1860s, on the back of the railway boom, a company bought the headland and converted the grand house to a hotel. Station Square and a network of 1500 building plots were laid out, with roads, drains and water mains. But potential investors did not relish being on top of a wind-swept cliff, with a long trek to a rocky beach, and the venture collapsed.

The views from Ravenscar have been appreciated for thousands of years. The dedication stone from the Roman Signal Station, which is now in Whitby Museum, reads: 'IVSTINIANVS P P VINDICIANVS MASBIER TVRRM CASTRVM FECIT A SO' The exact meaning has not been agreed; the Romans left the area in the early 400s.

Dinosaurs and ferns

The rocks of this part of the coast were formed in the Middle Jurassic period, when this was a coastline of mudbanks, fern forests and deltas. Dinosaurs lived here, and dinosaur footprints are found on the scar below Burniston, while Hayburn and Cloughton are famous for fossils of Jurassic plants.

Do not take fossils out of bedrock, just collect them from loose material. You can see dinosaur footprints and fine collections of fossil plants in Whitby and Scarborough museums.

Fine sandstone formed in river deltas was, for centuries, quarried at Cloughton for use in buildings in Scarborough and elsewhere.

Middle Jurassic fern

OUT AND ABOUT

 Six of the Best: Cloughton to Staintondale.

 Old Scarborough to Whitby Railway; bridleways across Staintondale.

 Cycle the Coast: Cloughton to Staintondale (online); Moor to Sea Cycle Network; old Scarborough to Whitby Railway.

WHERE ELSE CAN I SEE...

Alum works
Boulby alum works (access is restricted but visible from footpath); quarries at Kettleness, Sandsend, Saltwick and Carlton Bank.

HIGH MOORS *and* SOUTHERN DALES

The dales that run south from the great arch of the high moorland produce a series of spectacular landscapes. The beauty of the open moors is interrupted by swathes of vivid green (seen here at Rosedale) criss-crossed by stone walls and dotted with picturesque farmsteads. And as the dales run south they cut through the massive limestone plateau of the Tabular Hills, with its winding and endlessly beautiful northern escarpment. Here the dales change from bowls of pasture to wooded valleys, and the high ground moves from wild moorland to fertile farmland. This area, now serenely rural, carries evidence of a turbulent past, when ironstone and railways ended its isolation from the outside world.

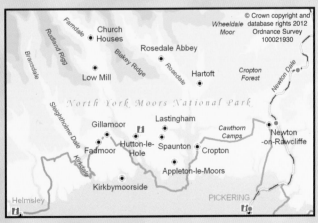

Fadmoor, Bransdale and Kirkdale

The moors, hills and streams of this area provide a continual series of fascinating and beautiful landscapes. Hodge Beck rises on the high moorland and cuts a series of dales running south through the moorland plateau and the Tabular Hills. Bransdale, Sleightholmedale and Kirkdale form a continuous valley but each has a distinctive character. The moors above the dales carry reminders of our Bronze Age past, while on a spur of the Tabular Hills sit the twin villages of Fadmoor and Gillamoor.

Fadmoor Water Race

Fadmoor and Gillamoor

Fadmoor is a collection of stone built houses around a lovely village green. Gillamoor is well-known for its 'Surprise View' – at its eastern end, the road turns sharply to reveal an enchanting view of Farndale. The little church was rebuilt single-handedly in 1802 by James Smith of Farndale, and an unusual four-faced sundial stands by the roadside in the centre of the village.

The two villages, situated on a high plateau of porous limestone, always had problems fetching and storing water. In 1747, a local engineer called Joseph Foord built open channels to bring water from the springs on the high moors to the north. But how could water get up the steep escarpment of the Tabular Hills? The whole plateau slopes down to the east and Foord was able to find points where the foot of the slope was higher than the villages, and then run sloping channels along the face of the bankside. Seen from the north the channels seem to be running uphill! Remnants of Foord's channels, including the foundations of an aqueduct on Pockley Moor, are still dotted across the landscape.

Bransdale

The long valley cut by Hodge Beck forms Bransdale, Sleightholmedale and Kirkdale. Bransdale is a gem; smaller and more remote than the dales on either side. There is no village here, just a scattering of farmhouses, together with a mill and a shooting lodge. In typical dales fashion the farmsteads are arranged half way up the daleside, just below the springline and regularly spaced around the dalehead.

The dale narrows going south into the wooded confines of Sleightholmedale,

ANCIENT WOODS AND TREES

Most of the natural woodland that once covered the North York Moors was cleared in prehistory so that, by Roman times, the familiar mix of woodland, moorland and farmland we see today was already present.

The most ecologically valuable are woods with unbroken links to the 'wildwood' - the primary woods. Woods that are at least 400 years old (and a few might be primary) are known as 'ancient woods'. They are some of our richest wildlife habitats and are important refuges for rare or less mobile woodland species, such as herb Paris or wood anemone.

Some ancient woods survived on steep ground, or where soils were too poor to farm. Many were managed intensively as coppices - often oak trees were grown for timber with an understorey of hazel, ash, alder or elm that was more regularly harvested for firewood, fencing and many other day to day needs.

Restoring native woodland and creating new woodland to strengthen the links across landscapes is now seen as vital for the continued survival of rare or specialist wildlife.

Walling in Bransdale

which cuts through the Tabular Hills, before entering a classic meandering floodplain at Kirkdale.

The moors in this area have lots of evidence of early settlement, including the barrows at Three Howes just east of Bransdale. The largest barrow was 25 metres long and was found to contain early Bronze Age pottery urns.

Bransdale Mill

Water mills were built by medieval lords of the manor to serve the farmers and to take a proportion of their grain as tax. Mostly small wooden buildings with no storage, many were converted to stone in the 18th century. By 1800 there was storage and dressing and rolling machines. Bransdale Mill was expanded from 1811 into a small complex. It is now owned by the National Trust and used for education, conservation and recreation groups.

Anglo-Saxon beads

Work and leisure

Conservation and leisure activities help to keep traditional trades busy. Stone walls need constant upkeep. Horse riding provides work for stables, saddleries, feed suppliers and farriers.

St Gregory's Minster

This ancient Saxon church stands isolated in Kirkdale, remote from any village. The main surviving Saxon features are the narrow arch from the tower to the nave and the celebrated sundial above the south doorway. The inscription on the sundial contains the message:

'Orm, the son of Gamal, bought St Gregorius Minster when it was all broken and fallen, and he has made it new, in the days of Edward the king and Tosti the Earl'.

This dates it to around 1060, just before the Norman Conquest.

The church is in a delightful setting, with a variety of woodland walks nearby.

The Saxon sundial at St Gregory's Minster

A Fadmoor farrier at work

OUT AND ABOUT

Tabular Hills Walk: Gillamoor-Fadmoor-Skiplam; Bransdale.

Monket House in Farndale to Rudland Rigg and Bransdale.

Rudland Rigg.

WHERE ELSE CAN I SEE...

Water mills
Surviving mills, some converted into houses, are dotted along the becks of many dales, including Thornton Beck, the Dove, the Rye and the Esk.

Pre-Norman churches
Ellerburn near Thornton-le-Dale, Hackness and Lythe all have carvings that predate the Norman conquest, while the crypt at Lastingham is very early Norman at latest.

Hutton=le=Hole and Farndale to Lastingham

Some of the most delightful and fascinating villages of the North York Moors lie on the Tabular Hills just east of Kirkbymoorside. Hutton-le-Hole, Appleton-le-Moors and Lastingham are each quite different, but all are steeped in a history that has given each village its unique shape and atmosphere. Rising above the villages is the great expanse of Spaunton Moor, topped by Ana Cross. Cutting through the moors on the west is the River Dove, forming the breathtaking valley of Farndale.

Hutton-le-Hole

Thought by the Victorians to be an 'ill-planned and untidy village', Hutton is now treasured for its open attractive layout. Back then it had a fierce reputation for drunkenness, fairs, cattle shows and cock-fighting.

This area was settled from the Bronze Age and had nearly 1,000 acres (400 ha) under cultivation by the time of the Domesday Book. Traditional farming and rural

Ryedale Folk Museum

crafts dominated until the Rosedale iron industry took off, with many miners lodging in Hutton. The open green was ideal for fairs and sports.

Now the village combines some farming with facilities for visitors, including the award-winning Ryedale Folk Museum. On an extensive site, the museum houses a collection of reconstructed buildings including cruck-framed long houses, a Tudor glass kiln, an early photographer's studio, craft workshops and farm buildings.

Hutton-le-Hole

The museum has also been part of the Cornfield Flowers Project, designed to conserve and revive flowers like blue cornflower, yellow corn marigold and shepherd's-needle that used to be common in arable fields.

Appleton-le-Moors

A near-perfect example of a planned medieval village, Appleton was laid out in the 12th century, probably by the new lord consolidating his land-holdings. The wide main street gives common grazing, while each house plot, or toft, runs to a back lane. The toft contained the tenant farmer's house, animal housing and barns. Each farmer also had a holding of around 15 to 30 acres (4 to 8 ha), with rights to gather wood and stone on the lord's estate. The effects of medieval planning, such as tofts and back lanes, rigg and furrow ploughing, and infield

Lastingham church crypt

MOORLAND CROSSES

and outfield systems, have been preserved all over the Tabular Hills.

Appleton Hall, the schoolhouse and the village church, with its distinctive French Gothic style, were all built in the 1860s by renowned architect J L Pearson.

Lastingham

The village is famous as one of the earliest Christian communities, and for its church crypt. An abbey was founded in Lastingham by St Cedd in 659 and flourished until it was destroyed by the Danes in the 9th century. William I decided to restore the abbey in 1078. Only the crypt and the apse of the church were completed before the monks left abruptly to set up a new monastery in York; the rest was completed in the 13th century. The crypt is one of the most impressive pieces of early Norman church architecture in England.

Spaunton Moor

This part of the moors, including the villages of Hutton and Appleton, were part of the medieval Spaunton Manor, given to the abbot of St Mary's Abbey in York by the Norman kings. The vast estate was sold off in pieces but the new owners retained ancient rights on the commons. The

Manorial Court Leet, a civil court dating back to medieval times, still meets annually. Spaunton Moor itself is, like much of the high moorland, managed for grouse shooting.

Farndale

The dale of the River Dove is sparsely populated, with just the tiny hamlets of Low Mill and Church Houses. But Farndale is a lovely place and, each springtime, the banks of the River Dove are carpeted with wild daffodils.

A special Daffodil Walk along the river links the two villages and, to help reduce congestion, a service of the Moorsbus network runs into the dale during the daffodil season.

At over 3 metres high Ana Cross (originally Ainhowe, or one-howe) is one of the tallest crosses on the moors. The head of the original Anglo-Saxon cross is in the church at Lastingham.

The 37 moorland crosses are a distinctive feature of the area, with a variety of names ranging from Young Ralph to Malo Cross and Fat Betty. Put up as way-markers and boundary posts from the Middle Ages onwards, they often stand on the junctions of old moorland trackways.

OUT AND ABOUT

 Tabular Hills Walk; Farndale Waymark Walk; Hutton-le-Hole to Lastingham and *Hutton-le-Hole to Lingmoor Waymark Walks*

 Gillamoor area, Lowna and up into Farndale; bridleway south of Hutton-le-Hole

 Rudland Rigg, Blakey to Blowath crossing.

WHERE ELSE CAN I SEE...

Planned villages
Carlton-in-Cleveland; villages on the southern fringe of the National Park at Middleton and Snainton; medieval tofts and back lanes are common, e.g. at Osmotherley and Hutton-le-Hole.

Moorland crosses
Because of their function as waymarkers, the crosses are spread across the high moors. There are good booklets giving the locations and histories of the crosses.

Blakey Ridge and Rosedale

Blakey Ridge and the Lion Inn are familiar features for travellers on the moors. The ridge carries the road from Hutton-le-Hole over the high arch of the central moorland to Castleton, its spectacular progress marked by the famous landmark of Young Ralph Cross and the always welcome sight of the Lion Inn. From the heights of the ridge, the long view down Rosedale is breathtaking. The scene is tranquil but a century ago Rosedale was an industrial centre, mining and processing iron ore in vast quantities. The remains of the ironstone trade are a fascinating reminder that, on the North York Moors, history is never far away.

The Blakey Inn

The use of the site of the Lion Inn (known to all as 'The Blakey') as a public house dates back to the mid-1500s, when land here was taken from Guisborough Priory by the Fevershams. In fact there may have previously been a friary inn here, run by monks. A market in the 1700s and the coming of the railway in the 1800s both sustained the inn, but the disappearance of the local iron mines was a blow.

Like many other moorland inns, the pub was made viable

Horseriding at Rosedale Cross

Young Ralph

The best known of all the moorland crosses (and symbol of the National Park) Young Ralph stands near the junction of roads to Westerdale, Rosedale, Castleton and Hutton-le-Hole. Legend has it that a Danby farmer named Ralph found a traveller who had died from exhaustion, and erected the cross as a memorial and guide to others. Rosedale Cross was put up above the village to mark the 2000 millennium.

Rosedale Abbey

Despite its name, the religious house in Rosedale was a small

Cistercian nunnery. It was established in the 12th century as a community of nine nuns and a prioress, and was closed in 1535. Stones from the priory were used in the village church, including the lintel over the north door with its carved motto 'Omnia Vanitas', All Is Vanity.

Near Rosedale look out for the outlier at Abbey Hill (a remnant of hard Jurassic sandstone sitting on top of softer rocks) and, at Northdale, the old pasture fields reclaimed by the moors.

Ironstone

Ironstone has been mined at Rosedale since medieval times, but large scale mining took off in 1856, promptly followed by the building of a railway. At Bank Top, south of the village, and along the east side of Rosedale, the remains of kilns are still visible, though mining stopped in the 1920s.

Ironstone Mine, Thorgill c. 1900

again by the arrival of the motor car, and one of the most remote and highest inns in England has thrived ever since as 'the pub on top of the world'.

ROSEDALE GLASS

Rosedale old railway track

The kilns were for calcining – iron ore was fired with coal to purify it and reduce its weight. The railway was divided into an upper section, for feeding the kilns, and a lower line, for tipping calcined ore into wagons. The line followed the dale sides and then made its way over the high moors to Battersby Junction, before the ore was taken on to steel works in Co. Durham and later Middlesbrough.

Iron mining was a big operation employing an estimated 2,000 people. The mine at Hollins Farm produced over 300,000 tonnes a year. Before then Rosedale was just a scattering of farms – the present village was largely built in the iron boom of the late 1800s. Other remnants include slag heaps and abandoned houses.

The Lion Inn

OUT AND ABOUT

 Walks around Rosedale Abbey.

 Bridleway from Hollins Farm to Lower Askew and over Spaunton Moor; bridleway north from Thorgill.

 Easy Going: Rosedale Mineral Railway (online).

WHERE ELSE CAN I SEE...

Industrial remains:
Remains of medieval iron mining at Bilsdale, Wheeldale, Westerdale, Rievaulx and elsewhere; later iron works were in lower Eskdale and on the coast near Port Mulgrave.

Monastic houses
Remains at Rievaulx, Byland, Mount Grace, there are also monastic remains at Whitby and Kirkham, just outside the National Park. Hackness and Lastingham have evidence of early Christianity.

Internationally renowned glassmakers established a glass blowing workshop in Rosedale several years ago, thereby reviving an old tradition.

Four hundred years ago, glass making was subject to a royal monopoly, and was largely carried out in secret. The mystery deepens because the Rosedale glass workers were Huguenots who had fled France – the strange language of these incomers, and their need for secrecy, made them seem highly exotic.

Their secret remained undiscovered for centuries, until their furnace was found on Spaunton Moor in 1968. In the 17th century, this was an ideal place for glass making. Timber was plentiful to supply heat for the furnace, local clay was used for crucibles, and the soil and rock provided silica and lime. The isolation was important for the Huguenot workers, who were breaking the royal monopoly.

The industry came to an end in 1615 when the need for shipbuilding led to a strictly enforced ban on burning timber. You can see a reconstructed glass furnace in Ryedale Folk Museum and visit the Rosedale glass workshop.

Cropton to Wheeldale Moor

The most westerly of the huge woods that clothe the slopes of the Tabular Hills is Cropton Forest, the largest in the area. The forest is mainly coniferous but there are delightful areas of broadleaved woodland too. The forest tracks, with stunning views over Newtondale, the moors, and the Vale of Pickering, are ideal for walkers, horse-riders and cyclists. On the southern edge of the forest are the lovely villages of Cropton and Newton-on-Rawcliffe, with the Roman site at Cawthorn camps in between. To the north are the open spaces of Wheeldale Moor, complete with a possibly Roman road.

Cropton Forest

With activity centres, camp sites and cabins tucked away among the trees, Cropton Forest is one of the National Park's best-kept secrets. Both Keldy Castle and Sutherland Lodge were built as 19th century shooting lodges; the former (now demolished) has holiday cabins in its grounds, the latter is an activity centre. The forest is a haven for wildlife, including badger, roe deer, fox, squirrel and hare, and a variety of woodland birds, reptiles, insects and wildflowers.

Keys Beck Ponds

Tucked away in the northern part of the forest, this lovely water feature is home to dragonflies, butterflies and occasional water-fowl such as teal. Spotted and marsh orchids and juniper, a rare sight in these parts, are all found here.

Cropton

Just north-west of the village stand the remains of a Motte and Bailey castle surrounded by a fence and still visible earthworks. The remains of a second ditch and earth bank that defended the castle approaches from the valley bottom are nearby. The Norman castle was founded by Robert de Stuteville to protect trade routes, and commands an excellent defensive position over Rosedale. The village was probably planned at the same time.

Cropton boasts its own brewery in the back of the pub, continuing a tradition dating back to 1613. Among the beers on offer is Scoresby Stout, marking Cropton's most famous son, the 18th-century Arctic explorer, and inventor of the crow's nest, William Scoresby.

Water and lime

Newton-on-Rawcliffe's village pond answered the need for a reliable supply of water on the porous limestone hills. In Hartoft Dale farm settlements dating back over 1,000 years, are dotted along the spring line. Lime was useful as a fertilizer and limekilns were common in these hills. Kilns at Cropton were last used in the 1960s.

Woolcraft

Local craftspeople are reviving old customs. Yarns, fleece rugs and felt using local wool are made at Wheeldale and elsewhere.

ABOVE LEFT: Keys Beck Pond
ABOVE: William Scoresby
LEFT: Common Hawker Dragonfly
BELOW: Hand-made woolcrafts

CAWTHORN CAMPS

The three fortifications at Cawthorn are among the most significant Roman sites in the region. Built around 100 AD, the forts seem to lie on a direct route between Malton (the Roman town of Derventio) and outposts on the east coast, while also commanding a high, dominant position between the territories of the Parisi and Brigantes.

Archaeologists believe there were two forts and a camp at Cawthorn, probably occupied at different times – the camp may have been used while one of the forts was being built. The surviving earth banks would have been topped by wooden stockades and the ditch around one fort was originally over 2 metres deep. The other fort had a second ditch added during a later occupation, serving to trap besiegers when the Romans counter-attacked.

The Romans withdrew in the fifth century; this extraordinary 2,000-year-old monument is a fascinating record of their occupation.

ABOVE: Cropton brewery beers
RIGHT: Wheeldale paved road

A Roman road?

An old road known as Wade's Causeway runs across the moors from north of Pickering to Grosmont, and possibly further. A paved section on Wheeldale Moor was uncovered in the early 20th century.

Originally thought to be Roman, because it passed near to Cawthorn camps, the standard of the work has led recent experts to believe it is either very late Roman, or, more likely, a medieval road. Either way, it is an intriguing sight.

OUT AND ABOUT

 Tabular Hills Walk: Newton to Cropton; Cawthorn Roman Camps Trail; Cropton Forest, Wheeldale Moor.

 Forest tracks in Cropton.

 Easy Going: Cawthorn Roman Camps (online).

WHERE ELSE CAN I SEE...

Roman remains
Goldsborough and Scarborough signal stations. Malton and York were major Roman centres; extensive Roman artefacts are in Malton Museum, the Yorkshire Museum in York, and Whitby Museum.

NEWTONDALE
and the
SOUTH EAST

The south east of the National Park takes in the extraordinary valley of Newtondale, the famous sights of Goathland and the Hole of Horcum, together with the forests of Dalby, Langdale, Broxa and Harwood Dale. The steam railway winds from Pickering to Grosmont, where it connects with the equally beautiful Esk Valley line. This is a wonderful way to visit Newtondale, Esk Dale and a host of villages.

The miles of forest tracks have long been enjoyed by walkers, horse-riders and cyclists; many parts of the forests are being converted to broadleaved woodlands, creating more wildlife habitats. The combination of wooded slopes, pastures and hidden valleys, makes this a very special area.

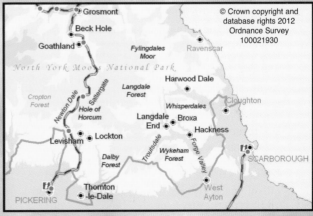

Goathland and Newtondale

As a village on the high part of the moors, Goathland's situation makes it unique, while its open layout is immensely attractive. The great gorge of Newtondale runs nearby and carries the secret of Goathland's prosperity. The coming of the railways turned poor isolated villages into desirable places to visit and live in, and brought industry to the North York Moors.

The railway runs through Newtondale, a stunning natural feature and one of the world's finest examples of a glacial meltwater channel. The revival of the steam railway gives visitors an ideal way to see and appreciate this beautiful landscape and its villages.

TOP: *Newtondale*
ABOVE: *Goathland Plow Stots*

Goathland
Villages in this area grew up where there was fertile soil, mostly on the Tabular Hills or in the dales, and many later expanded because of industry. Goathand is different. This lovely moorland village was for centuries a collection of scattered farms, scratching a meagre living from the poor soil and woodland. The arrival of the railway in 1836 brought waves of Victorian visitors eager to escape from smoky towns and cities. Ever since visitors have soaked up the charms of the village and its surroundings, including the waterfalls at Mallyan Spout, Thomasson Foss and Nelly Ayre Foss.

Plow stots
Plow Monday, the first Monday after Twelfth Night (6th January), is traditionally the day when ploughing starts again after Christmas. In Goathland the Plow Stots (men and women of the village) commemorate the day with music and dancing with swords that are ceremonially formed into a 'lock'.

Newtondale
The small stream and winding course of the gorge betray Newtondale's origins. Rivers and glaciers produce straight gorges with either a torrent or winding stream in the bottom. Newtondale was cut very quickly, so that the gorge actually winds with the stream. A small overflow from the glacial lake in Esk Dale soon turned into a torrent, but once the gorge had been cut and the lake drained, the little water that was left was captured by the Esk. The gorge is one of the finest examples of a glacial outflow channel in Britain, as well as being one of the National Park's most spectacular landforms. The present beck flows south and north from Fen Bog.

ABOVE: *Common Blue butterfly on Bird's Foot Trefoil* LEFT: *Old Locomotion Ale is a local brew* BELOW: *Access on the Rail Trail*

RAILWAYS

In 1836 the building of one of the world's earliest railways, between Whitby and Pickering, supervised by George Stephenson, was completed. To start with the carriages were horse-drawn, with the animals getting a free ride in a 'dandy cart' on the downhill sections! Steam locomotives arrived in 1845, but for 20 years the line was still interrupted by the famous Beck Hole incline. To make the climb up from the Murk Esk valley to the watershed at the top end of Newtondale, carriages were hauled up using an elaborate counterweight system. In 1865 an alternative route was engineered and a direct railway ran for the next 100 years.

The Grosmont to Pickering section was closed in 1965, but re-opened in 1973 as the North Yorkshire Moors Railway (NYMR). The refurbished steam trains are a delight to see and to ride on, and they give easy access to beautiful walking country. For a real railway outing, you can walk Stephenson's 1836 route from Goathland to Grosmont along the Rail Trail, and ride the train back.

The NYMR connects with the main line at Grosmont, giving access to Whitby, Esk Dale and beyond.

Mallyan Spout

number of these radiate out from the south of Scotland, reaching as far south as the North York Moors.

The Cleveland Dyke runs across the central part of the moors, creating a feature known as the Whinstone Ridge. The extremely hard rock, was used for paving stone, with many town and city streets being made of whinstone setts. The dyke has been quarried out to such an extent that the ridge is now a great trench across the landscape.

Habitats for wildlife

Unusual landforms often give rise to an interesting variety of habitats. The mix of habitats along Newtondale, from fen to moorland, pasture and forest, support a huge range of wildlife. Fen species, such as dragonflies, exist alongside excellent butterfly areas in Raindale and Raygate Slack. The forest tracks have lots of orchids, while the woods support a good variety of bird species. And the views, from Needle Point especially, are spectacular.

Skelton Tower

These romantic ruins, built in 1850 as a shooting lodge by the vicar of Levisham, are perched on the eastern edge of Newtondale. Some say the Reverend Skelton wrote his sermons here but it is also rumoured that he came to enjoy a quiet drink!

Whinstone

Around 60 million years ago movements in the earth's crust caused great splits to occur. These were filled with molten magma, which then solidified into vertical slabs of rock known as dykes. A

OUT AND ABOUT

 The Rail Trail; *Walks around Goathland*; use the railway for circular walks in and around Newtondale.

 Pedal and Puff leaflet for ways of combining outings on the North Yorkshire Moors Railway and cycling.

 Easy Going: Esk Valley to Beck Hole (online).

WHERE ELSE CAN I SEE...

Old railway routes
Scarborough to Whitby line at Hayburn Wyke, Hawsker and elsewhere is excellent for walking and riding; Rosedale mineral line, and across the moors to Ingleby; Whitby to Staithes line at Kettleness and elsewhere.

Thornton-le-Dale and Dalby Forest

One of the prettiest villages in Yorkshire, Thornton-le-Dale is well known for its lovely village green, its shops and the cottages stretching along the beck. Just north of the village is the tranquil valley of Ellerburn and the beginnings of Dalby Forest. This huge area of conifer and broad-leaved trees is open access land, and the Forestry Commission provides good facilities for walkers, horse-riders and cyclists. The real attraction though is the landscape and the combination of habitats that support a huge diversity of wildlife.

Thornton-le-Dale village

Thornton-le-Dale

As well as being picturesque, the village is of great historical interest. The market cross on the village green dates back to 1281, when Edward I granted the right to hold a weekly

RIGHT: Crossbills BELOW: Deer fawn in the forest

market to Thornton Manor. In 1657 Lady Lumley left provision for the building of a terrace of 12 almshouses, which still stand on the high street, each with one door and one window. The taller building at the end of the row was originally a grammar school. The turning on of the Christmas lights, with accompanying band and fair, and the summer show, are two of the notable traditions of Thornton-le-Dale.

Dalby Forest

From the 11th century a huge area of the Tabular Hills was made into a Royal Forest, with strict laws to protect deer and boar for the king to hunt. But by the 17th century the game

had declined and the forest was turned over to rabbit farming. These were specially bred for different coloured fur – the meat was a by-product!

Large-scale tree planting began in 1921 with mainly conifers for timber. Recent changes are seeing the gradual conversion of parts of Dalby Forest to native broadleaved trees like oak, ash, alder and hazel. Look out for signs of roe deer and badgers, as well as woodland birds like cross-bills and the elusive nightjar.

Within the forest there are ecosystems that provide habitats for special plants and animals. Deepdale, at the eastern end of the forest has limestone grassland species such as twayblade and the fragrant orchid. The waters of the White Beck deposit lime on rocks. Common lizards and butterflies such as the small pearl-bordered fritillary are seen here.

The forest caters for lots of activities, including dedicated mountain bike routes and a highwire forest adventure.

Pexton Moor

At the southern end of Dalby Forest, the Pexton Moor Trail from Haygate gives great views showing the diversity of

ABOVE: Adder RIGHT: Cycling in Dalby Forest

the forest. Here there are adders, lizards and a good mix of butterflies and birds including summer migrants like the garden warbler and blackcap. Ellerburn Bank Nature Reserve contains unimproved limestone grasslands with large numbers of cowslips, felwort and hairy violet being a notable feature.

Dalby village

The village at the centre of the forest has a nearby visitor centre, with information for walkers, horse-riders and cyclists, and about summer events. Dalby also has an astronomical observatory, with demonstrations.

The Bridestones

MILLS AND CHURCHES

Thornton Beck flows down a beautiful valley at Ellerburn. The waters were used to drive a series of paper mills in Ellerburn from 1680 until the late nineteenth century (the farms are named after the old mills). Now the beck feeds an extensive fish hatchery.

St Hilda's church, with its delightful setting, is one of the oldest in the area. The chancel arch and part of the nave date back to the time of the Norman Conquest. Older pieces, such as Viking carved stones, are embedded in some of the walls.

Pre-Norman elements of St Hilda's may have survived because, like St Gregory's Minster in Kirkdale, the church is positioned well away from any village.

Bridestones

Staindale lake is beautifully situated among the forest trees, and is near to the Bridestones – pillars of Jurassic stone eroded into spectacular shapes. They are in a Nature Reserve containing ancient woodland with an interesting diversity of wildlife.

OUT AND ABOUT

 Walks around Thornton-le-Dale; walks in Dalby Forest including Bridestones.

 Bridleway from Lockton to Givendale Head and Thornton-le-Dale; tracks in Dalby Forest.

 Moor to Sea Cycle Network; Good facilities in Dalby Forest.

 Easy Going: Staindale Lake in Dalby Forest (online).

WHERE ELSE CAN I SEE...

Old mills

Virtually every village had a water-powered corn mill, and many have survived as cottages or farms or, in the case of Bransdale mill, a visitor facility. Ruswarp mill was working until 1989.

Hole of Horcum and Levisham

A magnificent landscape feature, the Hole of Horcum has been formed by a series of springs slowly wearing away layers of limestone. South and west from here is Levisham Moor with views over Newtondale, and Levisham itself, a beautiful moorland village. Just to the north is Saltersgate Inn, where fish and smuggled contraband came over the moors from the coast, before being sent south to York.

Saltergate Brow and Malo Cross

A delightful walk due east from the Hole of Horcum takes you along Saltergate Brow. This is another section of the great escarpment that marks the northern edge of the hard upper Jurassic limestones of the Tabular Hills. As the path dips down you come to Malo Cross, bearing the initials RKE. Turn sharp right and you will walk past Blakey Topping, an outlier of upper Jurassic rock.

Lime-tolerant plants grow on the road side by the Hole of Horcum, but the slopes are acidic, supporting heather and bilberry. Down below the vegetation changes again, with meadows flourishing on the more fertile soils.

Old Salt Road

The old road from the coast became a famous route for smuggling, but the track was first made for fetching salt and fish (hence the name Saltergate). Salt was extracted from coastal salt pans and made into square blocks. You can see some salt boxes, used in homes for storing the square blocks, in the Ryedale Folk Museum.

The Old Salt Road was never paved, but it was used by wagons as it avoids the boggy parts of the moor. It runs roughly northeast from the Saltersgate Inn, meeting the Pannierman's Causeway at Lilla Cross before going on to the coast.

Lilla Cross

Stone crosses and markers are sited all over the moors,

ABOVE: *Hole of Horcum*
LEFT: *Blakey Topping*
BELOW: *Heather*

ABOVE: *Lilla Cross*
BELOW: *Neolithic flint scraper*

MOORLAND MANAGEMENT

Despite appearances, the moorland is not a natural landscape and about 5000 years ago was covered by forest. For centuries the moors have been grazed by sheep and today sheep farming and management for grouse shooting continue to maintain the landscape.

Between October and March small patches of heather are burned on an 8 to 15 year cycle to make a mosaic of heather of different heights. This provides habitat suitable for nesting and feeding for birds such as red grouse, golden plover and lapwing, with merlin selecting areas left unburnt for longer.

Without controlled burning and grazing, much of this fragile environment would eventually return to woodland with heather being a minor part of the ground flora.

where they were placed as way-markers or boundary posts. Lilla Cross is the oldest of all the moorland crosses, and the oldest Christian monument in the north of England. Dating from 626 AD, it commemorates Lilla, an officer of Edwin, king of Northumbria, who died on the spot where the cross stands, while saving the king's life.

As it stands on a round barrow, known as Lilla Howe, it is possibly a Bronze Age monolith, later carved into a rough cross.

Levisham Moor

Walking west then south from the Hole of Horcum takes you across Levisham Moor, with splendid views over Newtondale. This area is owned and managed by the National Park Authority. Levisham Moor remains much as it was 500 years ago, and holds the remains of human habitation going back over 3,000 years. Bronze Age barrows on the moor contained human remains together with pottery, tools and weapons; while ditched and banked enclosures date from the Iron Age. Though cultivated in the Middle Ages, this is now a mix of heather moorland, grass, and trees managed for nature conservation and recreation.

Levisham village

The path from the Hole of Horcum eventually leads to the village of Levisham. The wide main street, with grassed areas fronting the houses on both sides, has the classic layout of a planned medieval village. The road out of the village tumbles down to cross the beck near the beautifully situated St Mary's church. Danish sculpture here dates from the late tenth century, when Norse culture remained strong in this area. The alkaline waters of the beck encourage plants like ragged robin, lady's smock and globe flower.

Forge Valley, Troutsdale and Hackness

The southeast corner of the National Park holds some of its most delightful landscapes. Tucked away from the high moors, two enchanting valleys run through the eastern part of the Tabular Hills and meet at the village of Hackness. Forge Valley, which carries the River Derwent, is a wooded valley of great geological, historical and botanical interest. Troutsdale is beautifully secluded and winds through captivating scenery from the heights of Cockmoor Hall, with its extraordinary prehistoric dykes, to the tranquility of the valley floor.

ABOVE: Upper Jurassic Trigonia fossils LEFT: Forge Valley BELOW: Troutsdale

Forge Valley

This spectacular valley, a favourite for walkers, was formed during the last ice age by waters overflowing from a lake at Hackness. In modern times a canal or Sea Cut was built to take some of the Derwent Waters through to Scalby Beck. Raincliffe Woods lie along a spur of the main valley, and in the central section the Derwent winds through a wide level flood plain, where heron can be seen feeding.

The valley gets its name from the historic iron smelting industry, using charcoal from the surrounding dense woodland. The Derwent is a fine example of a clear lime-rich stream and Forge Valley Woods has been made a National Nature Reserve for its alkaline-rich flora. At the southern end of the valley the Derwent suddenly shrinks as half of its waters flow down into natural 'sink-holes', to fill the great aquifer that lies beneath the Vale of Pickering.

Geological trail

Forge Valley now has a specially-marked Geological Trail, starting at Old Man's Mouth, where you are guided through the different rocks of the Upper Jurassic period. The rocks of the valley were extensively quarried for building stone (especially the beautiful Hambleton Oolite), and for grinding stones (hence Whetstone Quarry). The quarries now provide splendid opportunities to see the Jurassic rock exposures.

Moors, including at Sawdon, just south of Troutsdale.

Prehistoric dykes

At the southern end of Troutsdale, near to Cockmoor Hall, there is a set of six banks and ditches running parallel for over 300 metres. These are part of a system of prehistoric dykes that is among the finest in England. The track running west from here crosses another set - Scamridge Dykes - that swings in a great arc from above Ebberston village to the head of Troutsdale, and there are further dykes to the south.

These late Bronze Age or early Iron Age structures were probably boundary markers between groups of people.

Hackness

The village of Hackness has a long and fascinating history. In 680 a nunnery was founded here as an outpost of Whitby Abbey. Parts of the present church date from the refounding of the abbey in the 11th century.

Margaret Hoby inherited Hackness estate in 1591; her journal is the earliest diary kept by an Englishwoman.

ABOVE: *Herons at nest* ABOVE RIGHT: *Crayfish from River Derwent*

Troutsdale

The name of this lovely valley, cut into the Tabular Hills by a series of springs and becks, has nothing to do with fish! It was originally named after a Viking called Trutr.

Raptor's Viewpoint in Wykeham Forest gives a view over Troutsdale that takes in the occasional bird of prey. Red kite, hobby, goshawk, buzzard and even honey buzzard and osprey have been seen here.

Heather honey is made all over the North York

WILLIAM SMITH

In the 1820s the pioneering geologist William Smith was given a job on the Hackness estate by Sir John Johnstone, a keen amateur naturalist. Smith had long dreamt of having a museum of geology, and Johnstone was able to raise funds for the building of the Rotunda Museum in Scarborough, which opened in 1829. This perfect building is made from sandstone quarried at Hackness.

OUT AND ABOUT

 Forge Valley Geological Trail; Tabular Hills Walk: Wrench Green to Crosscliff.

 Allerston to Wrench Green (UCR); Wykeham Forest; Baker's Warren.

 Moor to Sea Cycle Network.

 Easy Going: Forge Valley Woods (online).

WHERE ELSE CAN I SEE...

Prehistoric Dykes
The Cleave Dykes north of Sutton Bank; Casten Dyke; cross-ridge dykes on Levisham and Lockton Moors and on hills above Harwood Dale; Levisham Moor; Sproxton Moor; Danby Rigg.

Langdale to Harwood Dale

At the eastern end of the high moorland and Tabular Hills is an intoxicating mix of wooded plateaux and green valleys. The lime-rich soil gives good arable and pasture land at low levels, but the tops, previously a mix of scrub and moorland, have been extensively planted with conifers and broad-leaved trees. The result is a landscape of wide-open spaces and intimate valleys that has delighted generations of walkers.

ABOVE Moorcock Inn
RIGHT: Harwood Dale from Reasty Bank

Little Switzerland

Langdale was known locally as Little Switzerland because of its deep valleys and sudden steep hills. The village of Langdale End is surrounded by steep wooded and grass hillsides, including the slopes of Howden Hill. This curious small conical hill is a marvellous example of an outlier. All the banksides in this area are steep because a cap of hard rock (at about 170 metres above sea level) sits on top of bands of soft rock that are being eroded. On Howden Hill a cap of hard rock has survived, while all around it has been worn away; so the hill is an outlier, or survivor.

Long houses

The Moorcock Inn at Langdale End is a fine example of a long house. In these traditional houses, one portion was used for family living with another part, usually separated by a corridor, used for animals, feed and hay. The houses, generally one room deep, were extended by adding on rooms at either end.

Langdale Forest

This vast plantation is less developed for recreation than Dalby Forest, but some parts, including the upper reaches of the Derwent, are picturesque. The forests that stretch almost unbroken from Thornton-le-Dale to the coast at Cloughton, are full of wildlife, and there are special events held to see elusive wildlife such as badgers and nightjars.

Highs and Lows

Dales cut into the Tabular Hills by a number of streams run down to the village of Hackness and into the Derwent. Two of these dales, known as High Dales and Low

ABOVE: Tabular Hills from Howden Hill and Broxa
RIGHT: Nightjar

Badgers

Dales (which leads into the delightfully-named Whisperdales) lead up to Reasty Bank and the escarpment overlooking Harwood Dale. This is great walking and riding country, where the forest paths give grand views and the dales wind through captivating countryside.

Silpho

The villages of Silpho and Suffield sit on the high plateau of the Tabular Hills. The underlying limestone gives good soils for the farmers but is porous – rainwater drains through it. The water tower at Silpho and the numerous farm ponds, show the age-old need to preserve and store water on these hill-tops.

Harwood Dale

The village is a loose collection of farmsteads typical of the coastal belt. Just to the north are the ruins of St Margaret's church, an unusual example of early post-Reformation church architecture.

Between the village and the main Whitby to Scarbrough Road, and inside Harwood Dale Forest, is Standing Stones Rigg. Twenty-one stones were discovered here, forming an 8-metre circle. The forest on the south side of Harwood Dale is also rich in prehistoric 'tumuli', and the remnants of a prehistoric boundary at Thieves Dykes.

CHARCOAL

Many people are now looking to source food and other goods from their local areas. This has revived interest in customary ways of producing all kinds of things, and because so many customs have endured in the North York Moors, people here are at the forefront of this new approach. Local charcoal burners manage areas of woodland through coppicing and selected felling, and save us bringing barbeque charcoal halfway across the world! Coppiced wood is even being used in power stations.

Harwood Dale Forest is a large area of coniferous woodland, mainly pines and spruces, good for birdwatching and the ponds and ditches have interesting dragonflies.

Slacks and swangs

Running north from Harwood Dale village is a deep broad channel called Jugger Howe Slack. Originally formed during the last ice age by glacial meltwater, the valley carried water away from the edge of the North Sea ice sheet down towards Hackness. Meltwater channels are large depressions that now carry only small streams. They occur all over the moors, where they are known as slacks or swangs. Jugger Howe Slack is named after the howe, or round barrow, on the high ground to the east.

OUT AND ABOUT

 Upper Derwent Valley; Reasty Bank.

 Bridleways through Whisperdales, High Dales and Low Dales; Beacon Brow Road; Carr Lane; Broxa Forest.

 Moor to Sea Cycle Network.

WHERE ELSE CAN I SEE...

Slacks and swangs
In the last ice age Upper Eskdale was a series of lakes and outflow channels, including Lady Bridge Slack on Murk Mire Moor, Purse Dyke Slack, Moss Swang and Ewe Crag Slack. Coastal slacks include Biller Howe Dale Slack, Far Middle Slack and Nigh Middle Slack on Sneaton Moor.

Useful information

If this guide book has stimulated your interest in the North York Moors, there are lots of places to get further information about the National Park, much of it produced by the North York Moors National Park Authority.

Open Access
Open Access means that you can walk across miles of spectacular moorland that was previously out of bounds to the public. However you need to be aware of local restrictions. There is more information on the National Park website.

The main National Park information centres:

Sutton Bank National Park Centre
01845 597426

The Moors National Park Centre, Danby
01439 772737

There are mobile information centres parked at Farndale in the daffodil season and at the Hole of Horcum and Robin Hood's Bay in the summer.

There are Tourist Information Centres in and around the National Park in:
Guisborough
Helmsley
Pickering
Scarborough
Thirsk
Whitby

Places with visitor centres include:
Dalby Forest
Guisborough Forest
Hutton-le-Hole (Ryedale Folk Museum)
Ravenscar (National Trust Coastal Centre)

These villages have National Park Information Points:
Goathland
Grosmont
Osmotherley
Rosedale Abbey
Thornton-le-Dale

Internet
The North York Moors National Park website is well worth visiting. Go to www.northyorkmoors.org.uk.
The site holds vast amounts of information about the National Park. Click 'Discover the Place' and then 'Places of interest' to see an interactive map of the park.

Guides
Each year the National Park publishes *Out and About in the North York Moors*. It is available in the main visitor centres, or you can get one sent to you by ringing the Sutton Bank National Park Centre. Information on pubs, restaurants, cafés, shops, attractions, festivals, including agricultural shows, and events is available in these guides and from the centres listed above.

Art and artists
There are lots of artists living, working and selling their art in and around the moors, many of them using the landscape as their primary inspiration. Some artists' studios are open to the public and many artists enter the annual Open Studios weekends, usually held in June. In addition there are public and private galleries showing and selling local artists' work throughout the National Park.
The Inspired by... Gallery at The Moors National Park Centre runs a changing programme of work by artists inspired by the North York Moors.

Books
There are hosts of books and booklets about all aspects of the North York Moors, particularly walking guides, some produced by the National Park Authority and some by commercial publishers. For more in-depth reading on topics that have been touched on in this guide, the following are recommended

but should not be taken as a definitive list:

Robin A Butlin (editor) and Nick Staley (2003) *Historical Atlas of North Yorkshire*, Westbury
Detailed, highly illustrated account of North Yorkshire history with fascinating maps.

Roger Osborne (2010) *Rocks and Landscape of the North York Moors*, North York Moors National Park Authority
Illustrated guide to the fascinating ways in which rocks and landscapes are related.

Roger Osborne and Alistair Bowden (2001) *The Dinosaur Coast: Yorkshire Rocks, Reptiles and Landscape*, North York Moors National Park Authority
Illustrated guide to the geology of the Yorkshire Coast, aimed at general readers.

Nikolaus Pevsner (1966) *The Buildings of England: Yorkshire, The North Riding*, Penguin
Indispensable guide to notable buildings, including prehistoric monuments.

Peter F Rawson and John K Wright (2000) *Geologists Association Guide to the*

Yorkshire Coast, Geologists Association
More detailed geology guide for amateur enthusiasts and geologists visiting the area.

Royal Commission on the Historical Monuments of England (1987) *Houses of the North York Moors*, HMSO
Extraordinarily detailed and meticulous account of the vernacular architecture of the area, including farmhouses, barns, villages and town houses.

D A Spratt and B J D Harrison (editors) (1989) *The North York Moors Landscape Heritage*, North York Moors National Park Authority
An essential, expert and vivid guide to the development of the moors landscape, including

geology, farming, industry and tourism.

Nan Sykes (2008) *Wild Flowers of North East Yorkshire*, North York Moors National Park Authority
Beautifully illustrated, accessible guide to the flowers of the area.

Richard Vaughan (1974) *Birds of the Yorkshire Coast*, Hendon

Peter N. Walker (1990) *Folk Tales from the North York Moors*, Robert Hale

The Moors Message

There are over 1,400 miles (almost 2,300km) of paths and tracks across the North York Moors to help you discover even the quietest corner of the National Park. You can also walk on Open Access land (which is marked on Ordnance Survey maps) but you must look out for local restrictions.

Tread gently as in spite of surviving all sorts of weather, the moors, their plants and animals are fragile and sensitive.

Fences and walls keep some animals in and some out. Use stiles or gates and please leave gates as you find them.

Uncontrolled fires can devastate vast areas of moorland which may never fully recover. Don't start campfires or drop cigarettes or matches.

Litter is dangerous as well as unsightly. Take it home.

Dogs are permitted on rights of way but please keep them on a short lead. A loose dog can harm sheep and ground nesting birds. Dogs are not allowed on Open Access land in the North York Moors unless otherwise indicated on local signs.

Weather conditions can change. Mist on the moors is no fun. Are you fully equipped?

Footpaths are for feet. Bicycles and horses may be ridden on bridleways. Please remember that the countryside is shared and always consider others.

Take care at the coast. Stay away from the base of the cliffs; the rock is soft and cliff falls are common. Take local advice on the tides and make sure you don't get cut off.

Leave the countryside as you found it, for others to enjoy